Chris Billing was born in 1953 and
Wellingborough. While at Kingston Polytechnic
Northamptonshire he developed an interest in local buildings and their
history. Now an architect, his main interest in this respect is the
county's more unusual architectural follies, on which he had written
a dissertation whilst studying. The curiosities of the County have
provided an opportunity for another interest, as all but one of the
photographs are his.

Frontispiece
The Queen Eleanor Cross at Geddington (see No 13).

Northamptonshire Curiosities

Chris Billing

THE DOVECOTE PRESS

For Sally, David and Beverley.

First published in 1993 by the Dovecote Press Ltd
Stanbridge, Wimborne, Dorset BH21 4JD

ISBN 1 874336 12

© Chris Billing 1993
Phototypeset in Times by The Typesetting Bureau
6 Church St, Wimborne, Dorset
Printed and bound in Singapore

Contents

Introduction

Northamptonshire is blessed with numerous fine buildings, many constructed at a time of great affluence, producing a rich heritage of stately homes, churches and manor houses. Allied to these are the odd and the curious, collected or built either to satisfy some fanciful whim or to make a statement. Some 'curiosities' are based on tradition or found in folklore, whilst others attract theory and speculation due to their lack of factual evidence. There are no rules to define a 'curiosity' and, whilst my selection ranges the length and breadth of the county, it is inevitably compiled through personal choice.

Each 'curiosity' described in the text is identified by Ordnance Survey grid reference taken from the 1:50,000 Landranger Series, and includes a brief description of how to get there. Reference to the map and table of contents will identify other items in the immediate area, the closest of which are listed at the end of individual articles.

I am grateful to the many individuals and organisations who freely gave their time and encouragement in the daunting task of compiling this book. In particular, my thanks to the National Trust and English Heritage for allowing information from the guide books of Lyveden New Beild and the Triangular Lodge to be used. For the guidance of local historians and employees at public libraries and the Northamptonshire County Records Office, my gratitude. Also to the helpful staff of the Woodland Trust, the National Trust, English Heritage, the British Museum, Northamptonshire Museums, the Peterborough Diocesan Office, County Tourist Information Centres, the Lamport Hall Preservation Trust, the Sulgrave Manor Board and the estate offices of Althorp, Easton Neston, Castle Ashby, Boughton House and Milton Park.

My thanks also, to the various owners and custodians of other 'curiosities' for permission to take photographs, and to Mr. R. F. Sykes, Mr. M. Moser, Dr. S. Mattingly, Mr. J. Hadman, Mr. B. Moffatt, Mr. and Mrs. Marriott, Mr. S. Scott, Revd. P. R. Rose, Mr. J. Barker and Revd. R. D. Howe for supplying further supporting information. The photograph of the Volta Tower appears by kind permission of Mr. M. Palmer. I am also indebted for the support of my family and friends. Any success that this book may achieve is in no small measure due to the co-operation of you all.

Chris Billing
Wellingborough

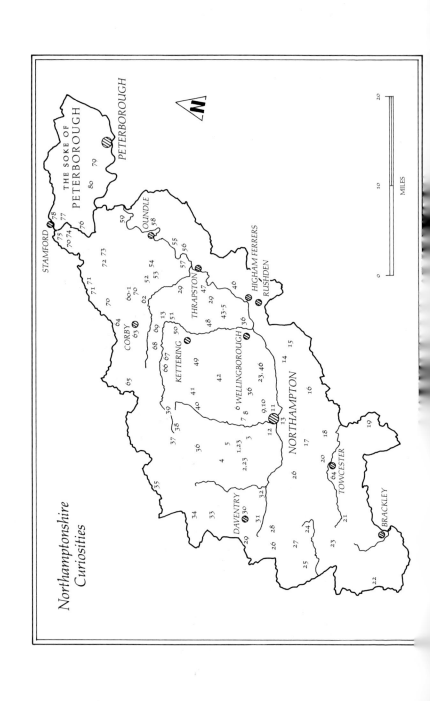

Northamptonshire Curiosities

1 The 'Be-Doing' Wood

Position: Althorp House.
OS Map: Northampton & Milton Keynes, Sheet 152.
Map Ref: SP683651.
Access: Althorp House lies approximately 4 miles north-west of
Northampton off the A428, Rugby Road. The house is open to the
public during the months of April and August only. Viewing of the
monuments is by prior arrangement only.

Althorp House became part of the Spencer family estate in 1508 when it
was bought by Sir John Spencer. Since then it has been considerably
enlarged by successive generations, and the grounds laid out with
woods and walks. One such planting became known by the unusual
name of the 'Be-Doing' Wood, and is still recognised as such today.

Running from the north-west corner of the house, an avenue of oaks
opposite beech trees was planted by the 2nd Baron Spencer in 1605. The
planting was recorded by a datestone, to which the avenue owes its
name. One side bears a shield and inscription, whilst on the other is
written: 'VP AND BE DOING AND GOD WILL PROSPER'

This datestone is the fourth in a series that so far totals seven, of

The 1901 tree plantation stone in the grounds of Althorp House.

which the most recent dates from 1901. No two are the same, but the stones of 1798 and 1800 are of unusual design. One is perched on top of the disused icehouse and consists of a cubic plinth supporting the base of a six feet high column. It is capped by a sphere on a spike, while the other similarly tall monument is capped by a carved stone pineapple.

Elsewhere in the grounds stand an obelisk dedicated to the memory of Margaret, Viscountess Althorp, and a brightly coloured wooden temple which originally stood in the grounds of the Admiralty in London.

Places of Interest in the Neighbourhood
  2. An Aviation Landmark (Little Brington)
  3. A Manorial Roost (Upper Harlestone)
  5. The Largest House in All England (Holdenby)
23. Famous American Ancestry in Northants (Little Brington, Althorp)

The spire of St John, Little Brington.

2 An Aviation Landmark

Position: Little Brington.
OS Map: Northampton & Milton Keynes, Sheet 152.
Map Ref: SP664634.
Access: 5 ½ miles west of Northampton and east of Daventry, Little Brington stands to the north of the Roman road between Duston and Whilton, between Flore and Great Brington.

Standing in the corner of a large field is the tall tower of the former Church of St John. Built in 1856 by the 4th Earl Spencer, it was constructed as a Chapel of Ease for those at Little Brington and nearby Nobottle who found it difficult to attend services at Great Brington.
   By the end of the Second World War St John's had become unused and neglected, and so, during 1947 its gradual demolition began. Before completion however, the Air Ministry asked that the tower and spire be spared as they appeared on RAF maps and were used as a landmark by their pilots! Thus the tower and spire were saved and stand today as a monument to the generosity of the 4th Earl.

Places of Interest in the Neighbourhood
  1. The 'Be-Doing' Wood (Althorp)
  3. A Manorial Roost (Upper Harlestone)
23. Famous American Ancestry in Northants (Little Brington, Althorp)
32. In Anticipation of Napoleonic Invasion (Weedon Bec)

3 A Manorial Roost

Position: Upper Harlestone.
OS Map: Northampton & Milton Keynes, Sheet 152.
Map Ref: SP693640.
Access: Situated within 1 mile of the north-western fringe of
Northampton, Harlestone is on the A428 with Upper Harlestone to the
south-west, on the Great Brington road. The curiosity is the last
building on the left in the village and stands in the front garden of a
private house next to the former village laundry.

Originally built as the dovecote of the Lumley Manor Estate, it used to
be said by the village folk that this delightful structure was as old as
the church rebuilding work in nearby Harlestone. That would make it
early 14th century and while it still contains 440 nesting holes for
pigeons, its conversion in 1848 was to the picturesque garden store of
its current use.

Places of Interest in the Neighbourhood
  1. The 'Be-Doing' Wood (Althorp)
  2. An Aviation Landmark (Little Brington)
  5. The Largest House in All England (Holdenby)
23. Famous American Ancestry in Northants (Little Brington, Althorp)

The picturesque dovecote at Upper Harlestone.

4 From Pump to Tower

Position: East Haddon.
OS Map: Northampton & Milton Keynes, Sheet 152.
Map Ref: SP667682 and SP669682.
Access: 7 miles north-west of Northampton, East Haddon lies just off
the A428 road to Rugby. Both curiosities are accessible from the minor
road through the centre of the village.

East Haddon is fortunate in retaining two structures charting the
development of its communal water supply. The earlier of the two is the
19th century water pump and rustic shelter which stands to one side of
the Holdenby road at the junction of a narrow lane heading south.

   The second is to be found opposite the church in the back garden of
the post office. Here stands the village water tower, similarly circular
with a conical roof, but this time altogether more substantial. Built of
stone in 1890, it rises some twenty-five feet to the eaves where a water

The village water tower at East Haddon.

level indicator once hung so as to show when a top-up was necessary. Inside, and approximately three feet above the former floor, is the base of a circular water tank which rises the full-height of the tower.

When first built, the daily task of filling the tank with a hand pump was undertaken by the local blacksmith. An inertia pump was later installed, supplying water to the tank until 1956 when the village was connected to the mains. It is now a curious local landmark from a bygone age.

Places of Interest in the Neighbourhood

One of the 'Base Court' arches of Holdenby House.

5 The Largest House in All England

Position: Holdenby.
OS Map: Northampton & Milton Keynes, Sheet 152.
Map Ref: SP694676.
Access: 5 ½ miles north-west of Northampton, Holdenby lies on the minor road between East Haddon and Church Brampton and between the A428 and A50.

In the tiny village of Holdenby once stood what is reputed to have been the largest house in all England. It was built by Sir Christopher Hatton between 1570 and 1582, and was 120 yards long and 74 yards wide. All that now remains are indications of landscaping, and two curious stone archways which stood to the east of the house.

Standing to the north and south of a flat square of land known as the 'Base Court', each arch is flanked by empty alcoves and capped by a trio of incomplete pinnacles. A third arch is incorporated in the approach to the present house and may have been constructed from remains of the mansion, which was partially demolished within 80 years of its construction. During its brief existence it was visited by Queen Elizabeth I, sold to James I in 1607, and imprisoned the captured Charles I.

The present house was constructed in the 1870s and 80s, and opens to the public on certain days between Easter and September.

Places of Interest in the Neighbourhood
  1. The 'Be-Doing' Wood (Althorp)
  3. A Manorial Roost (Upper Harlestone)
  4. From Pump to Tower (East Haddon)
23. Famous American Ancestry in Northants (Little Brington, Althorp)

6 The Ruin on the Green

Position: Boughton to Moulton road.
OS Map: Northampton & Milton Keynes, Sheet 152.
Map Ref: SP763655.
Access: From the village of Boughton, just off the A508, take the sign-posted road to Moulton. Within 3/4 mile, the ruins appear on the left and the Green on the right. The churchyard is kept locked, but the ruins may be seen from the boundary wall.

East of the village of Boughton are the ivy-clad remains of the old church dedicated to St John the Baptist. Ruinous since at least 1724, the church and its graveyard stand on the edge of a roughly triangular plot of land known as Boughton Green, once the site of an ancient fair which became the largest horse market in the Midlands.

King Edward III granted a Royal Charter to the fair in 1351, permitting three days of trading and festivities to take place towards the end of June. Such were its location, timing and length that the fair became immensely popular, attracting custom from near and far. At the end of the 19th century, its importance declined in the face of alternative trading markets and the event lost support. In 1916 it was abolished and its 565 year history came to an end, leaving the church to quietly decay.

Places of Interest in the Neighbourhood
7. An Unwelcome Obelisk (Boughton)
8. The Castellated Follies of Boughton
9. William Shakespeare's Tree (Abington)
10. The Well in the Tower (Abington)
36. The Pytchley's Proud Past (Pitsford, Brixworth, Overstone)

The ruined church of Boughton Green

7 An Unwelcome Obelisk

Position: Boughton.
OS Map: Northampton & Milton Keynes, Sheet 152.
Map Ref: SP754652.
Access: Heading north from Northampton on the A508 Harborough road, turn right opposite the hospital into Holly Lodge Drive. Take the first left into Obelisk Rise and follow the road up the hill to the summit where the obelisk is on the left.

More than one obelisk has been constructed in Northamptonshire, but the earliest appears here at Boughton, on what is undoubtedly the highest piece of land in the village. Built in 1764 to the memory of William Cavendish, 4th Duke of Devonshire, the obelisk rises some hundred feet – to the considerable annoyance of the farmer on whose land it stood. He completely obliterated the inscription at its base, it is said, because of the damage visitors inflicted on his crops in the surrounding fields.

Today, this majestic local landmark finds itself surrounded by Northampton's expansion, with housing around much of its base, and shows serious signs of decay.

Places of Interest in the Neighbourhood
   6. The Ruin on the Green (Boughton Green)
   8. The Castellated Follies of Boughton
   9. William Shakespeare's Tree (Abington)
  10. The Well in the Tower (Abington)
  16. The Pytchley's Proud Past (Pitsford, Brixworth, Overstone)

The obelisk at Boughton.

8 The Castellated Follies of Boughton

Position: Boughton.
OS Map: Northampton & Milton Keynes, Sheet 152.
Map Ref: SP749660, SP768662 and SP770669.
Access: Boughton lies about 3 miles north of Northampton, just off the A508. From the village take the signposted roads to Moulton for a mile or so, where Holly Lodge appears on the right and Spectacle Lane is opposite.

In the late 18th century the 2nd Earl of Strafford indulged in an architectural flight of fancy, applying castellations to most if not all the buildings on his estate, including the original Manor House.

Most easily seen of the remaining follies is the Hawking Tower, which stands as an entrance lodge on the A508 and forms a small dwelling. Built in the style of a church tower, it is remarkably similar to Steeple Lodge at Wentworth Castle in South Yorkshire, which was built in the 1730's by the 1st Earl. Elsewhere, remain two catellated farm buildings and a crude grotto enclosure built in a spinney around a natural spring.

To the east on the estate, by the side of Spectacle Lane, is a castellated arch known as 'the Spectacle' or 'Spectacles'. Built as an ornamental feature on the Moulton Parish boundary, it was copied and incorporated into nearby Holly Lodge, built some hundred years later. Here an archway and a pair of turrets form an entrance gateway to a utilitarian yard with a high, fortified wall frontage. The main house also has castellations, whilst to the rear a tall tower supports a steeply rising curved roof. The entrance to the house, now a private residence, is also from the Boughton road, via a unique pair of cast-iron gates made with the forms of a dozen agricultural implements.

Places of Interest in the Neighbourhood
  6. The Ruin on the Green (Boughton Green)
  7. An Unwelcome Obelisk (Boughton)
  9. William Shakespeare's Tree (Abington)
 10. The Well in the Tower (Abington)
 36. The Pytchley's Proud Past (Pitsford, Brixworth, Overstone)

The castellated arch of Spectacle Lane.

9 William Shakespeare's Tree

Position: Abington Park, Northampton.
OS Map: Northampton & Milton Keynes, Sheet 152.
Map Ref: SP775616.
Access: Abington Park lies approximately 1 ½ miles east of the centre of Northampton, adjacent the A4500, Wellingborough road.

The former manor house acts as a focal point to a number of curiosities, both natural and man-made (see No 10), but of greatest significance are the associations with William Shakespeare. These began in the mid-17th century when his sole descendant, Elizabeth Hall, and her husband, lived at the Manor for more than twenty years. The Manor then passed to the Thursby family who, a little over a century later, introduced a further connection.

Anne Thursby had long been an admirer of the works of Shakespeare and had become a close friend of Garrick, the celebrated Shakespearian actor of the day. Together they had obtained a cutting from the Mulberry tree growing in Shakespeare's own garden at New Place, Stratford-upon-Avon, which he is reputed to have planted and refers to in a number of his writings. The cutting was planted at the centre of the east lawn where it still stands today, its low slung branches twisted with weight and age. For a number of years the tree bore a crescent shaped brass plate recording the planting in February 1778.

Places of Interest in the Neighbourhood
10. The Well in the Tower (Abington)
11. The King Versus the Archbishop (Northampton)
12. In Praise of King Charles II (Northampton)
13. The Queen Eleanor Crosses (Hardingstone)

10 The Well in the Tower

Position: Abington Park, Northampton.
OS Map: Northampton & Milton Keynes, Sheet 152.
Map Ref: SP777618, SP774619 and SP781617.
Access: Abington Park lies approximately 1 ½ miles east of
Northampton, adjacent the A4500, Wellingborough road.

Upon its sale to the Thursby family in 1669, the Manor House was
virtually rebuilt, leaving only its foundations and some inner walls. The
Thursbys also built a tower to the north-east of the Manor House,
inside which is a well once served by a waterwheel and stairs leading to
a dovecote above. Access for the birds may be seen at mid height on the

William Thursby's tower in Abington Park.

western side, whilst elsewhere the tower bore William Thursby's initials and the date.

Shortly after the tower's completion, work began on Archway Cottages in the north-west corner of the park, two symmetrical pairs of cottages connected by a high archway. A further smaller arch stood to the east. Acting as a spurious gateway to the park, it was formerly castellated, with a low wall between the gatepiers. The arch has now collapsed, leaving only the piers.

Places of Interest in the Neighbourhood
 9. William Shakespeare's Tree (Abington)
11. The King Versus the Archbishop (Northampton)
12. In Praise of King Charles II (Northampton)
13. The Queen Eleanor Crosses (Hardingstone)

Becket's Well in Northampton.

11 The King Versus the Archbishop

Position: Northampton.
OS Map: Northampton & Milton Keynes, Sheet 152.
Map Ref: SP749604 and SP760603.
Access: Both curiosities are close to the centre of Northampton, the Gateway by the side of the road into town from Daventry/Rugby near the railway station, while the Well enclosure is on the Bedford road from the A45.

Northamptonshire is studded with historic monuments, while the county town, having suffered a disastrous fire in 1675, has lost much to record its importance – despite once having both a university and a castle in which no less than eight parliaments were held. It does however have two similar curiosities, both modest in design, recalling the town's part in what was to become one of the most shameful events in English history. For it was here, in 1164, that Henry II forced a confrontation with his Archbishop of Canterbury, Thomas a Becket, which eventually led to Becket's murder by four of Henry's knights five years later.

The king had forced Becket to trial on a minor charge, from which the Archbishop was acquitted. Further charges were brought, which Becket resisted, and eventually the king was forced to order his barons to find him guilty of treason. As the Earl of Leicester began to pronounce sentence, he was interrupted by an outburst from the Archbishop, who then made his escape.

The traditional account records his leaving the castle by the Dern Gate and stopping at a nearby well before making his way, disguised as a humble priest, to the Northamptonshire woodlands of the north.

All that remains of the castle is a re-erected gateway built into a stone wall near the railway station. To the east is Becket's Park, and adjacent on Bedford road, a similar arched enclosure of 1843 records the location of Becket's Well.

Places of Interest in the Neighbourhood
  9. William Shakespeare's Tree (Abington)
 10. The Well in the Tower (Abington)
 2. In Praise of King Charles II (Northampton)
 3. The Queen Eleanor Crosses (Hardingstone)

12 In Praise of King Charles II

Position: Northampton.
OS Map: Northampton & Milton Keynes, Sheet 152.
Map Ref: SP754605.
Access: The monument stands at the very heart of Northampton, in front of All Saints Church on an island surrounded by Mercer's Row, Wood Hill, George Row and The Drapery.

Following his defeat by the Parliamentarians in 1651, the future King Charles II fled north into Shropshire. As the search for him intensified, he is reputed to have sought refuge in an oak tree. Disturbed by troops searching for him, a flock of birds in the tree took flight, leading the parliamentary forces to ignore the branches overhead as a possible hiding place for their quarry.

From that day forth, May 29th has been celebrated as Oak Apple Day, with various traditions developing in different parts of the country. In Northampton, a statue of King Charles II is decorated with a garland of oak leaves. The monument was erected in 1712 to record the king's gift of 1000 tons of timber from the nearby forest of Whittlewood and that of seven years chimney-money, donated to All Saints Church and the town following the fire of 1675.

Chimney-money was an unpopular tax of 2/- on every fireplace in a property, which Charles II had introduced. Its return in the wake of the fire might therefore be seen as an appropriate gesture.

Places of Interest in the Neighbourhood
 9. William Shakespeare's Tree (Abington)
10. The Well in the Tower (Abington)
11. The King Versus the Archbishop (Northampton)
13. The Queen Eleanor Crosses (Hardingstone)

13 The Queen Eleanor Crosses

Position: Hardingstone and Geddington.
OS Map: Northampton & Milton Keynes, Sheet 152. Kettering &
Corby, Sheet 141.
Map Ref: SP754582 and SP895830.
Access: The Hardingstone Cross is 1 mile south of Northampton's town
centre, on the A508. Geddington lies 2 miles north of Kettering and 3
miles south of Corby, off the A43. The Cross is at the heart of the
village on the road to Grafton Underwood.

The Eleanor Crosses of Hardingstone and Geddington are familiar
landmarks within the county (for illustration of the Cross at
Geddington see frontispiece), but little is known of the Queen in whose
memory they were erected. Eleanor of Castile was the wife of Edward I
(1272-1307), and the royal couple frequently visited the royal hunting
lodge at Geddington, which once stood to the north-east of the church.
She travelled with him on numerous occasions, but in 1290, whilst the
king's army headed north to fight the Scots, she was taken ill and died.
So distraught was Edward that all plans to attack the Scots were
abandoned, and a mournful procession began its 150 mile journey
south from Harby in Nottinghamshire to Westminster, where she was
buried on 17th December.
  Sometime later, Edward I issued instructions that each resting place
on the route be provided with a stone cross as a lasting tribute to his
Queen. Erected at Lincoln, Grantham, Stamford, Geddington,
Hardingstone, Stony Stratford, Dunstable, St Albans, Waltham,
Cheapside and Charing Cross ('chere-reine' – 'dear queen'), no two
crosses were alike, Hardingstone's having been luxuriantly painted
from base to pinnacle. Only three survive: the two in Northamptonshire
and Waltham Cross in Hertfordshire. The monument at Charing Cross
is a copy erected on the site of the original.

Places of Interest in the Neighbourhood
11. The King Versus the Archbishop (Northampton)
12. In Praise of King Charles II (Northampton)
16. On the Toss of a Coin (Horton)
17. England's Longest Navigable Canal Tunnel (Blisworth)

14 Of Buildings, Bee-hives and Balustrades

Position: Castle Ashby.
OS Map: Northampton & Milton Keynes, Sheet 152.
Map Ref: SP862592, SP855572 and SP862613.
Access: About 7 miles east of Northampton, the house may be reached from the A428 by taking the road through Yardley Hastings, and following the signs to the house. This route crosses the south avenue from the house before heading to the village.

The curiosities in the house and grounds at Castle Ashby have evolved over many years, but the earliest is possibly its most famous. The parapet balustrade around the roof is in the form of lettering, reproduced in Latin and taken from Psalm 127. Dated 1624 and probably the work of Inigo Jones, very few examples exist in the country, and only one, in Norfolk, predates this rare feature.

In the 19th century garden terraces contained within yet more balustrade lettering were laid out in the grounds. The architect Sir Matthew Digby Wyatt is thought to have been involved, as he is known to have designed the curious water tower to the west of the house, in 1865. Elsewhere, to the south of the church, Sir Matthew was also employed on designs for bee-hives. Here, two enclosures were built to house the hives in two rows of five each. Sadly, the hives have long since been removed, but the stone fragments that remain give an indication of their former grandeur.

Another architect to work on the garden buildings was Edward Godwin who, in 1868-70, had built the symmetrical entrance screens on either side of the road between Denton and Yardley Hastings. Godwin was also commissioned to provide designs for a further lodge to the north of the estate, where the picturesque Station Lodge now terminates the view along the road from Earls Barton.

Places of Interest in the Neighbourhood
15. Rustic Buildings on the Bridleway (Easton Maudit)
16. On the Toss of a Coin (Horton)
23. Famous American Ancestry in Northants (Ecton)
46. Scratch Dials (Ecton)

Station Lodge at Castle Ashby.

15 Rustic Buildings on the Bridleway

Position: Easton Maudit.
OS Map: Northampton & Milton Keynes, Sheet 152.
Map Ref: SP889585 and SP870590.
Access: Easton Maudit is 8 miles east of Northampton and 5½ miles south of Wellingborough on the minor road between Grendon and Bozeat. A single track lane links the village with its neighbour, Castle Ashby, where a distant view of Nevitt's Lodge may be seen from the road between Grendon and Yardley Hastings.

Just off the main road through Easton Maudit is a short terrace of two storey stone cottages which curiously end with a single storey building quite unlike any other in the village. Built of stone with a thatched roof supported on crude knotty tree trunks, the wide overhang provides a porch or veranda to each of its three sides. It is positioned at the

The curious rustic cottage at Easton Maudit.

intersection of a lane and bridleway which leads west to Castle Ashby House. By the gateway pillars into the grounds of the House is a second thatched cottage, 'Nevitt's Lodge', with a similar veranda and rustic columns. A third rustic work, the circular' Knucklebone Arbour', has a conical thatched roof supported on slender wooden columns and a floor decorated in a petal pattern formed in sheep's hooves.

Undoubtedly from the early 19th century, all three are linked to the Castle Ashby Estate, where the recently rediscovered diary of Lady Alwyn, sister-in-law to the 3rd and 4th Marquis of Northampton, tells us that Nevitts Lodge was formerly called 'Derbyshire's Lodge' (after a coachman) and that Knucklebone Arbour was formerly 'Margaret's Bower', in honour of the 2nd Marquis's wife. Frequent reference to the 1st Marchioness, and the certainty that it was she who instigated a small bridge on the estate, has led to the suggestion that the rustic works might also be hers. Although no proof has yet come to light, the atribution seems both feasible and sensible.

16 On the Toss of a Coin

Position: Horton.
OS Map: Northampton & Milton Keynes, Sheet 152.
Map Ref: SP825545 and SP828542.
Access: 5 miles south-east of Northampton, Horton lies on the B526 to Newport Pagnell. From Horton, follow the signposted route towards Denton but taking the village road to the right where the Denton road bends sharply to the left. The buildings are on the right.

To the east of Horton down a narrow lane is Temple House (once New Temple) which at first appears to be little more than a traditional two storey house. The hidden view to the south-west, however, is one of a splendid classical portico, set against the impressive backdrop of well-established trees. To complement New Temple, a triumphal arch stands further down the lane on the edge of an adjacent field. These and one other surviving building were all built as eyecatchers to the now demolished Horton Hall of Lord Halifax, who had been financially ruined within ten years of his support for an unsuccessful candidate to the Parliamentary elections of 1768.

A three-cornered fight had taken place between candidates supported by the Earls Halifax, Northampton and Spencer of Horton, Castle Ashby and Althorp respectively. The collective cost to the three of them has been estimated at £160,000, although their lavish expenditure only resulted in a tie, with the final decision being made on the toss of a coin!

As a consequence of his losses, Lord Halifax forfeited his estate to the Government, and Horton Hall was finally demolished in the 1930's. The Arches and New Temple remain, both of which may be viewed across the parkland from the B526.

Places of Interest in the Neighbourhood
13. The Queen Eleanor Crosses (Hardingstone)
14. Of Buildings, Bee-hives and Balustrades (Castle Ashby)
15. Rustic Buildings on the Bridleway (Easton Maudit)

17 England's Longest Navigable Canal Tunnel

Position: Blisworth/Stoke Bruerne.
OS Map: Northampton & Milton Keynes, Sheet 152.
Map Ref: SP730528 to SP739503.
Access: About 5 miles south-east of Northampton, Blisworth is on the A43. Follow the road signs to Stoke Bruerne which is just off the A508, about 7 miles south of Northampton.

To the west of the road linking Blisworth to Stoke Bruerne is a series of seven chimney-like structures, each circular but of differing heights. Some are obvious, standing tall by the roadside, while others are partially hidden in hollows and vegetation. They run in a perfectly straight line almost parallel to the road and identify the route of the Grand Union Canal through the Blisworth Tunnel. From its start in 1793, the tunnel's 3075 yard length took more than ten years to construct, and it is the airshafts which may now be seen by the roadside.

Canal boats of this era relied upon horses to pull them. Once inside a tunnel, progress depended on 'leggers'; men who lay on top of the boats

Ventilation shaft to the Blisworth canal tunnel.

and 'walked' the tunnel sides or roof for its entire length. In Blisworth Tunnel, fresh air was originally provided by four airshafts. Later, with the introduction of steam as a method of propulsion, two men were fatally overcome in the tunnel by a build-up of noxious gasses, and by 1881, three additional air shafts had been provided to improve ventilation.

At the official opening of the canal the tunnel had remained incomplete, having been abandoned in 1797 due to construction difficulties. Tunnelling finally recommenced in 1802, and now, almost two hundred years later, it remains the longest navigable tunnel on the British Waterways system.

Places of Interest in the Neighbourhood
13. The Queen Eleanor Crosses (Hardingstone)
18. The Stoke Park Pavilions (Stoke Bruerne)
20. To the Memory of 'Pug' (Easton Neston)
26. One of England's Finest (Bugbrooke)

The formal setting of the Stoke Park Pavilions.

18 The Stoke Park Pavilions

Position: Stoke Bruerne.
OS Map: Northampton & Milton Keynes, Sheet 152.
Map Ref: SP740488.
Access: 3 miles east of Towcester and 7 ½ miles south of Northampton, Stoke Bruerne stands on minor roads between the A43 and A508. To find the pavilions, travel south from Blisworth as far as the T junction, with Stoke Bruerne to the left and Shutlanger to the right. Immediately opposite is a single track lane which continues for about 3/4 mile through Stoke Park Wood and on to the pavilions beyond. Opens to the public during June, July and August at weekends only.

The village of Stoke Bruerne is well-known locally for its canal boat trips and waterways museum. Perhaps less well-known is the existence at Stoke Park of a pair of elegant pavilions, standing on a stepped garden terrace and framing an extensive view across the Tove valley. Built of contrasting cream limestone and dark brown ironstone, their construction in 1629 must have raised some controversy, as they are probably the earliest examples of an Italian 'Palladian' style in the country. Inigo Jones is credited with their design, although their builder, Sir Frances Crane, who had been given the manor in payment of a debt, could just as easily have brought the designs back from Italy. When the pavilions were added to the existing manor house, they provided a chapel and library. The Tudor manor at the centre was to be replaced with one in matching style, but Sir Frances's death brought the project to a halt. The centre section was eventually adapted and refaced to match the pavilions, but was burnt down by a fire in 1886.

In 1953, having been allowed to go derelict, a scheme for work to the pavilions was published in *Country Life*, whereupon they were bought by the present owner and restored. The result is one of isolated splendour, a fragment of architectural magnificence caught in unspoilt countryside.

Places of Interest in the Neighbourhood
7. England's Longest Navigable Canal Tunnel (Blisworth)
9. A Trio of Canal Curiosities (Cosgrove)
0. To the Memory of 'Pug' (Easton Neston)
4. In Search of Charles Dickens (Towcester)

19 A Trio of Canal Curiosities

Position: Cosgrove.
OS Map: Northampton & Milton Keynes, Sheet 152.
Map Ref: SP793427. SP793425 and SP800418.
Access: 7 miles south-east of Towcester and 5 miles west of Newport
Pagnell, Cosgrove lies almost on the county boundary with
Buckinghamshire. From Old Stratford, take the A508 heading north
for about ½ mile before turning right and into Cosgrove. The second
right leads to the tunnel curiosity with the other two within easy
walking distance.

The 1793 Act of Parliament sanctioning construction of the Grand
Junction Canal created problems for the canal company engineers.
Tunnelling at Braunston and Blisworth tested their abilities, and a trio
of canal curiosities at Cosgrove bear witness to their ingenuity.

  Built in two halves and meeting here at Cosgrove, one requirement of
the canal was that the main street, which lay across its route, should be
kept open. Eventually, the road had to be re-routed over a new ornately
carved stone bridge to the north. A pedestrian tunnel beneath the canal
completes the route of the former street. Referred to by some as a
packhorse tunnel, this narrow passage is barely high enough to stand
upright, and is approached by steps to its horseshoe-shaped entrances.

  To the south of the village the canal formerly stepped down the sides
of the Great Ouse Valley, before crossing and climbing back up the
other side into Buckinghamshire. Problems with winter flooding
required the canal to be raised on a forty feet high man-made
embankment, almost a mile long and linked over the river by a
three-arched stone aqueduct. This opened but collapsed within three
years to be replaced by a cast iron aqueduct which opened in 1811.
Known as the 'Iron Trunk', it is some 101 feet long, 15 feet wide and
stands 36 feet above the river.

Places of Interest in the Neighbourhood
18. The Stoke Park Pavilions (Stoke Bruerne)
20. To the Memory of 'Pug' (Easton Neston)
64. In Search of Charles Dickens (Towcester)

20 To the Memory of 'Pug'

Position: Easton Neston.
OS Map: Northampton & Milton Keynes, Sheet 152.
Map Ref: SP703496 and SP704477.
Access: 1 mile north-east of Towcester, Easton Neston House is
approached from the A43 where the village of Hulcote is signposted.
The House is not generally open to the public and prior arrangement
should be made with the Estate Office (Tel. 9327 50969) for viewing.
The entrance to the racecourse is off the A5, just south of Towcester.

Of Easton Neston village only the Church of St Mary remains, and that
now stands amidst the formal gardens of Easton Neston House, the
family home of Lord Hesketh.
   Probably from about the same time as the House of 1685, a delightful
temple faces across an expanse of lawn towards the church. Inside,
supported on two carved slabs of stone bearing representations of
rearing horses and a standing hound, is a third slab recording the death

The commemorative trestle within the Temple at Easton Neston.

of a pet dog. The inscription reads:

To the Memory of PUG who
departed this Life June ye 24th 1754
in the third Year of her Age.

No Blazon'd Coat or Sculptur'd Bone,
(Honours we scarcely deem our own)
Adorn this simple rustic Stone
But Love & Friendship without Blame,
With Gratitude we justly claim;
Where will Faith ever find the Fame?
Not unlamented now she dies:
Besprinkled here this Tribute lies
With heavenly Tears from Angels Eyes.

Elsewhere at Easton Neston is the glorious entrance screen of 1822, now the entrance to Towcester Racecourse, and adorned with deer above the end lodges.

Places of Interest in the Neighbourhood
17. England's Longest Navigable Canal Tunnel (Blisworth)
18. The Stoke Park Pavilions (Stoke Bruerne)
26. One of England's Finest (Bugbrooke)

Remnants of Astwell Castle.

21 Astwell Castle

Position: Helmdon.
OS Map: Northampton & Milton Keynes, Sheet 152.
Map Ref: SP609441.
Access: Helmdon is 4 miles north of Brackley and 7 miles south-west of
Towcester at the intersection of a number of minor roads linking
Wappenham, Weston, Sulgrave, Greatworth and Syresham, north of
the A43.

East of Helmdon, the narrow road to Wappenham crosses a small
bridge over a tributary of the River Tove. To its south is a curious stone
tower with a collection of smaller buildings around its base. These are
the remains of a once substantial 15th century fortified manor house,
now known as Astwell Castle.

   In 1586 the estate became the property of George Shirley who made
significant alterations, possibly involving some demolition work. He
created a courtyard house of which the tower was only a small part, and
above whose central gated arch he inserted a stone bearing his coat
of arms, his initials and a date of 1607. Only a small portion of his
mansion remains. Now a private house, it may be viewed from a distance or by prior arrangement.

Places of Interest in the Neighbourhood
22. St Rumbold's Well and Replica (Astrop)
23. Famous American Ancestry in Northants (Sulgrave)

22 St Rumbold's Well and Replica

Position: Astrop.
OS Map: Stratford-upon-Avon, Sheet 151.
Map Ref: SP508364 and SP508362.
Access: 5 miles west of Brackley and 3½ miles south-east of Banbury, head south from the A422 towards Charlton. Follow the signs west to Newbottle and King's Sutton where the replica well is by the side of the road. Head north from King Sutton on the Upper Astrop Road for 3/4 mile to Astrop House. The well is on private property and viewing is by consent only.

In one of the hollows on the edge of a small spinney in the grounds of Astrop House stands St Rumbold's Well, the only surviving remnant of a once thriving centre for the relaxation of the wealthy. Its waters were discovered in the mid-17th century to be rich in minerals, and in 1668 were described as able to achieve miraculous cures for a variety of complaints.

The popularity of Astrop Spa spread, and by 1740 it boasted landscaped grounds, tea rooms, an assembly hall and long wide gravel walks with benches. No plan exists of the spa in its hey-day, when there were weekly balls and all the accessories of a fashionable watering place. Within thirty years, however, the spa, lodging houses and assembly hall were reported to be in decline and eventually closed.

The land on which the well-head stands was sold in 1866 to Sir William Brown on the condition that a replica well-head be built in such a location as to provide public access to its waters. This was duly carried out, and the facsimile of the ornamental well-head now stands in a depression by the side of the road to Newbottle. To distinguish it from the original, it is called Astrop Well, although the water was always considered inferior, and for a time no water could be seen at all! Recent repairs to St Rumbold's Well have restored the flow.

Places of Interest in the Neighbourhood
21. Astwell Castle (Helmdon)
23. Famous American Ancestry in Northants (Sulgrave)

St Rumbold's Well at Astrop before restoration.

23 Famous American Ancestry in Northamptonshire

Position: Ecton, Sulgrave and Little Brington.
OS Map: Northampton & Milton Keynes, Sheet 152.
Map Ref: SP828634, SP562456 and SP663636.
Access: Ecton lies south of the A4500, Northampton to Wellingborough road; Sulgrave to the north of Brackley by the B4525: Little Brington west of Northampton between the A45 and A428. Sulgrave opens to the public every day except Wednesday from the beginning of March to the end of December.

Northamptonshire has become a place of pilgrimage for many visitors from the United States of America who wish to trace the family origins of two of America's Founding Fathers. Benjamin Franklin's family may be traced back to the village of Ecton, where it had owned a farm and bell foundry for 300 years and ran the village smithy. The grave of his uncle and aunt may be seen in the graveyard, whilst on the north wall of the church is a further commemorative tablet.

At Sulgrave Manor may be traced the ancestry of George Washington, where, during the 16th century, Lawrence Washington twice held the office of Mayor of Northampton. In 1656, his great-great grandson, John Washington, emigrated to Virginia and founded the estate now known as Mount Vernon. His great-grandson, George, was born in 1732 and, after driving out the English during the War of Independence became first President of the United States.

The manor was sold by the family shortly after John's emigration. His great-uncle however had built a more modest residence in the village of Little Brington, which still stands by the southern tip of the village green. Brasses in the Church of St Mary, Brington, record the deaths of Robert and Elizabeth Washington and bear the family coat of arms, which was later to evolve into the American flag.

Places of Interest in the Neighbourhood
  1. The 'Be-Doing' Wood (Althorp)
  2. An Aviation Landmark (Little Brington)
 21. Astwell Castle (Helmdon)
 46. Scratch Dials (Ecton)

24 The Priory's Legacy

Position: Canons Ashby.
OS Map: Northampton & Milton Keynes, Sheet 152.
Map Ref: SP579506 and SP579508.
Access: Canons Ashby is 7 miles south of Daventry on the B4525. The
well stands on private property, but can be viewed from the road into
the village, while the church is open to the public.

To the north-east of the village is a curious stone structure which dates
from 1253 when the nearby Augustinian priory was granted a license to
enclose a well. It has an arched entrance, vaulted ceiling and wooden
pipes leading to the Manor House, from where water was drawn until
as recently as the 1950s.

   A further priory remnant is the distinctive church of St Mary, of
which all but the 14th century tower and two bays of the nave and north
aisle were destroyed at the time of the Dissolution.

Places of Interest in the Neighbourhood
23. Famous American Ancestry in Northants (Sulgrave)
25. The Unfortunate John Merrick (Redhill Wood)
26. One of England's Finest (Charwelton)
27. Railway Relics (Woodford Halse/Hinton)

The former Priory church of St Mary, Canons Ashby.

25 The Unfortunate John Merrick (the Elephant Man)

Position: Redhill Wood.
OS Map: Stratford-upon-Avon, Sheet 151.
Map Ref: SP508512.
Access: 7½ miles north-east of Banbury and 9 miles south-west of Daventry, Redhill Wood is just off the A361. The farmhouse is now a private residence but may be seen across open fields from the road.

On the A361, just before the road descends into Chipping Warden, an insignificant track leads off between fields towards an isolated farmhouse. Here was found the hospitality and seclusion required for the unfortunate John Merrick, otherwise known as the 'Elephant Man', who stayed as a guest of Lady Knightley from nearby Fawsley Hall.

Merrick first came to attention appearing in a freak show of the 1880s. So grotesque were his deformaties that the sensation seekers who paid to see him frequently fled in a state of distress. His existence became known to the eminent physician, Sir Frederick Treves, who befriended Merrick and studied his condition. A letter appeared in *The Times*, telling Merrick's story, who Treves had discovered to be both highly sensitive and intelligent. As a consequence, many people befriended Merrick, who began to feel more accepted, but imprisoned by his two room lodgings in the London Hospital.

One such visitor was Lady Knightley, who provided him with both Redhill Farmhouse and the peace and seclusion of the nearby wood. Whilst here, Merrick wrote many appreciative letters to his newly found friends, but his happy time in Northamptonshire was short. With his condition worsening, he returned to hospital in London, where he died in April 1890.

Places of Interest in the Neighbourhood
23. Famous American Ancestry in Northants (Sulgrave)
24. The Priory's Legacy (Canons Ashby)
26. One of England's Finest (Charwelton)
27. Railway Relics (Woodford Halse)

26 One of England's Finest

Position: Charwelton.
OS Map: Northampton & Milton Keynes, Sheet 152.
Map Ref: SP535561.
Access: 4½ miles south-west of Daventry, Charwelton and the bridge are on the A361 road to Banbury.

At Charwelton, recent road improvements have thankfully preserved a small bridge which crosses the trickling River Cherwel. Measuring about three feet wide and four feet high, this small stone bridge dates to a period when the transportation of goods relied upon the sturdy backs of horses, and has been described as one of the finest surviving pack-horse bridges in England.

   A second Northamptonshire packhorse bridge may be found at Bugbrooke (SP673568), about 5 miles south-west of Northampton.

Places of Interest in the Neighbourhood
27. Railway Relics (Woodford Halse/Hinton)
28. The Three Curious Buildings of Fawsley Park

The packhorse bridge at Charwelton.

27 Railway Relics

Position: Woodford Halse/Hinton.
OS Map: Northampton & Milton Keynes, Sheet 152.
Map Ref: SP541525.
Access: 5½ miles south of Daventry, the neighbouring villages of Woodford Halse and Hinton stand on minor roads south of Charwelton and north-west of Moreton Pinkney, and between the A361 and B4525.

One of the purposes of the late-19th century Great Central Railway was to link the industrial Midlands with Europe via a Channel tunnel. Woodford Halse, in it's central location, was earmarked to play a key role at the junction of rail links to all parts of the country. By 1899 buildings, sidings, platforms and a station had been built.

The cross Channel tunnel has arrived too late to save the Great Central, which was closed in the 1960s. What does remain are a number of curious leftovers, such as concrete columns and beams rising from a garden, a pair of semi-circular arched blue brick bridges and an over-sized half timbered building in Hinton, now used as the Woodford Halse Social Club.

The two villages are joined by the route of the former railway, whose north and south bound tracks once thundered over the bridges. The road beneath is still called Station Road, whilst the Social Club was formerly the Railway Hotel. The strange lumps of concrete are the remains of platform supports built on the side of embankments to the rear of the Station Master's house. This is now the home of a family who might easily look upon living there as something of a family tradition. Both the great-grandfather and uncle of the occupants served as Station Master, and both once lived in the house.

Enthusiasts of the Great Central Railway still meet on a monthly basis in the Social Club, where a model records the layout of the railway complex as it appeared in its heyday.

28 The Three Curious Buildings of Fawsley Park

Position: Fawsley Park, Preston Capes and Badby.
OS Map: Northampton & Milton Keynes, Sheet 152.
Map Ref: SP570579, SP573547 and SP554585.
Access: Fawsley Hall is approximately 3 miles south of Daventry. For the Dower House take the minor road south from Newnham, past the first left turn to Everdon and up the hill. At the top, opposite farm buildings on the left, is a gate into the parkland. The Dower House remains are about ½ mile west. The eyecatcher faces Church Wood from the high ground in Preston Capes, midway between Maidford and Charwelton. The Lantern House stands by the side of the A361, ½ mile south of Badby.

With the death of Sir Edmund Knightley of Fawsley Hall in 1542, his widow took up residence in the Dower house. Dating from the early years of the 16th century the brick and stone building was once impressive, with a castellated tower and tall chimneys each of different designs. Last inhabited in 1704, it is now almost entirely covered with ivy, but remains the earliest example of brick building in the county.

The Lantern House just outside Badby.

Sadly, after standing derelict for almost 300 years, it may soon be unrecognisable as a house at all.

The second curiosity is an architectural folly built in the nearby village of Preston Capes. Here, near the summit of a steep rise, is a pair of formerly symmetrical cottages separated by an arch and decorated with castellations. Its construction was intended to act as an eyecatcher when viewed from the grounds of the Hall.

The third curiosity is known as Badby Lantern House and is a two storey octagonal house of stone. After lying derelict, it has recently been restored and extended to make a modern house of considerable charm. The original work dates from the same era as that at Preston Capes, and it is thought that Thomas Cundy, who extended the Hall in 1815/16, was employed on both.

Places of Interest in the Neighbourhood

The circular toll-house at Sudborough.

29 Toll Houses of Old England

Position: Staverton, Sudborough and Twywell.
OS Map: Northampton & Milton Keynes, Sheet 152.
  Kettering & Corby, Sheet 141.
Map Ref: SP554618, SP972822 and SP953782.
Access: 1 mile south-west of Daventry, the toll house at Staverton
stands in a lay-by off the A425. The one at Sudborough, 3 miles
north-west of Thrapston, is at the eastern end of the village near the
A6116. The toll house at Twywell is the last building on the right when
travelling towards Woodford. All are now private residences.

In medieval times roads consisted of little more than dirt tracks which
remained waterlogged and deeply rutted for most of the year. The
13th century introduction of toll roads was designed to improve their
quality. But it wasn't until the 17th and 18th centuries that Acts of
Parliament formalized the arrangements and established a network
covering the country. Groups of men, principally the landed gentry,
were appointed turnpike trustees. They employed toll-keepers to collect
the fees, authorised expenditure for road repairs and shared in the
profits from their use. During the early 19th century, Northamptonshire was crossed by up to 36 turnpikes, a high number for so small a
county.
  Payment of fees, particularly for agricultural implements in
predominantly rural Northamptonshire, proved exceedingly unpopular
and the toll-keepers occasionally found themselves under attack.
Weapons were frequently kept by the front door, whilst windows were
strategically positioned and often protected by sturdy iron bars.
  The houses were built in all shapes and sizes, be they circular as at
Sudborough, rectangular with a bay end as at Twywell, or a wide 'V'
as at Staverton. Here, a single storey entrance lobby is set across the
internal angle with tall, narrow windows at either side of the door.
Directly facing the former road and toll-gate, it is an excellent example
of the defensive 'front door'.

Places of Interest in the Neighbourhood
Staverton: 30. The Unintentional Eyecatcher (Daventry/Newnham)
  31. Two Garden Delights (Newnham)
Sudborough/Twywell: 47. An Unexpected Find (Woodford)
  48. The Wellington Tower (Burton Latimer)
  57. A Masonic Plaque (Aldwinkle)

30 The Unintentional Eyecatcher

Position: Daventry/Newnham.
OS Map: Northampton & Milton Keynes, Sheet 152.
Map Ref: SP575610.
Access: At the intersection of Daventry's ring road and the A45 from
the east, take the road towards the town centre and then first left as
signposted to Newnham. The curiosity is on the right.

Travelling around Daventry, the motorist's eye is invariably attracted
towards an isolated structure standing high on the summit of Burrow
Hill. Once a windmill, its modern reconstruction has echoed the design
of its former roof, which is believed to have been a ten sided pyramid.
Built approximately two hundred years ago near the site of an earlier
mill, it continued in operation until the mid 1880s. After a period of
dereliction,it was purchased by the local Water Authority, who sold it
to the present owner in 1984. Following restoration, it is now used for
watching wildlife on the adjacent 'Beggar's Bank'.

Places of Interest in the Neighbourhood
28. The Three Curious Buildings of Fawsley Park
29. Toll Houses of Old England (Staverton)
31. Two Garden Delights (Newnham)
32. In Anticipation of Napoleonic Invasion (Weedon Bec)

The former windmill on Burrow Hill.

31 Two Garden Delights

Position: Newnham.
OS Map: Northampton & Milton Keynes, Sheet 152.
Map Ref: SP584603 and SP583596.
Access: 1 mile south of Daventry and 10 miles west of Northampton, Newnham lies on the B4037 with the Hall to the north-east of the church. The grounds of the Hall are open to the public on one day of the year only, usually in April, in aid of the National Gardens Scheme (phone 0483 211535 for details). The Nuttery is open throughout the year.

In the grounds of Newnham Hall is a small moated island and an ivy-clad sham ruin dovecote of 19th century origins. Nearby stands an even smaller structure which may have been an ice-house. It seems likely that the pair were intended to be in clear view from the Hall, but today, their accidental camouflage and the haphazard way in which one stumbles on them make them even more intriguing.

Elsewhere, at the far end of Manor Lane, is a great rarity for a Northamptonshire village. Behind high walls and established for over 200 years is 'The Nuttery', 2.3 acres of hazel coppice underplanted with snowdrops and daffodils. It was acquired by the Marriott family in 1820, who harvested the cob-nuts for marketing at Covent Garden and Coventry. The heart of the coppice has recently been donated to the Woodland Trust, in whose care this fading aspect of British history is maintained.

Places of Interest in the Neighbourhood
28. The Three Curious Buildings of Fawsley Park
29. Toll Houses of Old England (Staverton)
30. The Unintentional Eyecatcher (Newnham)
32. In Anticipation of Napoleonic Invasion (Weedon Bec)

32 In Anticipation of Napoleonic Invasion

Position: Weedon Bec.
OS Map: Northampton & Milton Keynes, Sheet 152.
Map Ref: SP629594.
Access: Weedon Bec is 4 miles south-east of Daventry and 7 miles west of Northampton at the crossing of the A45 and A5. The depot is in the centre of town.

When faced with a traditional portcullis one expects to be standing at the entrance to a castle, not a small Georgian building – such as the one at Weedon Bec.

   During the reign of George III Northamptonshire's pivotal importance as a central shire county was once again recognized. It was also established that as well as being the furthest point from any coastline, Weedon Bec had superb communication links with London. As a result,

The gatehouse of the Royal Military Depot at Weedon Bec.

when the country was under threat of invasion by the French during the Napoleonic Wars at the start of the 19th century, work began on the construction of a Royal Military Depot on the northern valley slope of the Nene. The group of buildings formerly comprised 12 large stores for powder magazines, barracks for two regiments, and a group of buildings in which the Royal family could take refuge. A branch of the newly opened Grand Junction Canal projected into the centre of the group, forming a wharf, and it is across this that one of the two buildings with a portcullis forms a nautical gateway. The second may still be seen at the far end of the wharf.

Places of Interest in the Neighbourhood
26. One of England's Finest (Charwelton/Bugbrooke)
30. The Unintentional Eyecatcher (Daventry/Newnham)
31. Two Garden Delights (Newnham)

The gatehouse at Ashby St Ledgers.

33 Home of the Gunpowder Plot

Position: Ashby St Ledgers.
OS Map: Northampton & Milton Keynes, Sheet 152.
Map Ref: SP572681.
Access: Ashby St Ledgers lies 3 miles north of Daventry, and ½ mile east of the A361 road to Rugby. The Manor House is next to the village church, from where the gatehouse may be viewed.

'Bonfire night', 'Fireworks night', and 'Guy Fawkes night' all refer to the celebrations held on November 5th, but only the latter title retains a link with the origins of the festivities. The inhabitants of Northamptonshire, however, have an added cause for remembrance, as two notable county families were deeply implicated in the events of 1605.

In Ashby St Ledgers, Robert Catesby motivated and inspired his fellow conspirators in meetings held at the timber-framed gatehouse which spans the Manor House carriageway. From here, the plot was orchestrated to drive a shaft beneath the House of Lords, pack it with explosives and detonate it during the opening of Parliament.

To raise funds, Catesby contacted Francis Tresham of Rushton, who had recently inherited his father's fortune, and who impulsively pledged £2000 to the conspiracy. It was his involvement however, which was eventually to lead to the conspirators downfall. Unnerved by all he stood to lose, Tresham wrote the letter betraying the plan, which in turn led to the discovery of Guy Fawkes and the barrels of explosives.

Upon hearing of Guy Fawkes's arrest, Catesby and five others rode north to Ashby St Ledgers to inform the waiting conspirators of the plot's failure. The group dispersed, but were rounded up or killed in ensuing fights. The initial list of conspirators did not include Tresham, and it is likely that he was implicated by those who had been caught. Later arrested and imprisoned in the Tower of London, he died in December 1605. He had not been indicted, but shared the fate of his fellow conspirators with his corpse being cut up, his head exhibited and his lands confiscated by the crown.

Places of Interest in the Neighbourhood
24. The Kilsby Towers
29. The Pytchley's Proud Past (Wetton)

34 The Kilsby Towers

Position: Kilsby.
OS Map: Leicester & Coventry, Sheet 140.
Map Ref: SP570708 and SP572705.
Access: Kilsby is 4 miles south-east of Rugby and 5½ miles north of Daventry at the junction of the A5 and A361.

On the southbound side of the A5, rising out of the dip which now bypasses Kilsby, stands an immense tower. Within ¼ mile on the opposite side of the road, is an equally impressive second tower – cleaner perhaps, but identical in all other respects to the first.

They each measure sixty feet in diameter and are approximately a hundred feet deep, ventilating the railway tunnel which passes beneath. The tunnel, constructed at the height of the Victorian railway boom,is 2423 yards long and was once the longest tunnel intended for steam trains. It was built for the London and Birmingham Railway in the 1830s, and almost £100,000 was set aside to cover the costs. Opponents of the scheme feared that passengers travelling in the open coaches would be overcome and suffocate in the darkness. Consequently, the two large towers were designed to provide ventilation.

Unforeseen obstacles in its construcstion included running water and quicksand. Steam pumps capable of pumping 1800 gallons per minute were manned by navvies labouring from floating rafts, but it still took nineteen months before the quicksands were overcome. Eventually, in the spring of 1838, behind schedule and over budget, a passenger service was started, although for a few months it depended upon coaches and buses running from Denbigh Hall, to Rugby.

Recent strong winds caused masonry from the top of one of the towers to fall on the busy line beneath. The result was the complete restoration of the second shaft, which is why it now appears in such splendid condition.

Places of Interest in the Neighbourhood
33. Home of the Gunpowder Plot (Ashby St Ledgers)
35. 'Icaro Alteri' (Stanford-on-Avon)

35 'Icaro Alteri'

Position: Stanford-on-Avon.
OS Map: Leicester & Coventry, Sheet 140.
Map Ref: SP593793.
Access: 5 miles north-east of Rugby and 15 miles west of Kettering,
Stanford-on-Avon stands on the county boundary between the A14 and
B5414. The monument is in a field about ½ mile to the north-east of the
village.

A surprising monument to be found in Northamptonshire is that in a
field on the north-western boundary, where a small classical column
stands as a memorial to pioneer aviator Percy Sinclair Pilcher.

A full four years ahead of the Wright Brothers' historic first powered
flight, the 32 year old Pilcher had constructed his fifth glider, and undertaken trials of the engine he proposed fitting to it. During the summer
of 1899 the Hon. Adrian Verney Cave provided a base for Pilcher and

The Percy Pilcher monument at Stanford-on-Avon.

his experimental flying machines at Stanford Hall. From here, Pilcher made several successful flights in his fourth glider, 'The Hawk', which was made of bamboo, pine and fine sail cloth. As a way of raising funds, a demonstration was arranged for September 30th, and an audience invited to watch. In spite of frequent light showers and gusty winds on the day, Pilcher successfully took off and reached a height of 60 feet. Those watching suddenly heard a loud snap. The glider's tail collapsed, it's wings folded upwards, and it crashed to the ground, leaving Pilcher unconscious. Pilcher died two days later, and was buried in Brompton Cemetery in London.

Proposals to erect a monument in the park were immediately put forward. Yet it required a public appeal for funds some eleven years later before work commenced in 1912. The base of the monument carries two inscriptions: 'Percy Pilcher, Pioneer of Aviation, Fell Here September 30 1899' and 'Icaro Alteri' (Another Icarus).

Places of Interest in the Neighbourhood
33. Home of the Gunpowder Plot (Ashby St Ledgers)
34. The Kilsby Towers
37. 'To Commemorate that Great and Decisive Battle' (Naseby)
38. The Copper Ball and Iron Jug (Naseby)

The archway to Pytchley Hall, now at Overstone Hall.

36 The Pytchley's Proud Past

Position: Overstone, Welton and between Pitsford and Brixworth.
O.S. Map: Northampton and Milton Keynes, Sheet 152.
Map Ref: SP797661,SP594662 and SP750688.
Access: The arch at Overstone Park is 4 miles north-east of
Northampton and east of the A43 at the junction of minor roads
between Moulton and Overstone. The smaller monument is 2½ miles
north-east of Daventry, east of the B4036 by the entrance to Welton
Grange Farm, the larger monument is between Pitsford and Brixworth
on the A508.

Foxhunting in Northamptonshire attained notoriety when in the late-
18th century John, Earl Spencer, founded a hunting club at Pytchley
Hall. The lavish hospitality enjoyed by the forty privileged members,
combined with hunts over fortnightly periods, soon made the Pytchley
Hunt famous. The club survived for about sixty years, whilst the Hall
was pulled down in 1828 and the village road driven across its site.
Fragments were removed to Sulby, Glendon and elsewhere, but most
notably to Overstone Park, where the main entrance archway was

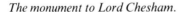

The monument to Lord Chesham.

enlarged with side gates and re-erected to the north-west of Overstone Hall.

   Standing near Welton Grange, a memorial cross is inscribed to mark the spot where one of the Pytchley Hunt's members fell and died in 1907. The inscription is now misleading however, as the monument has been moved from its original location by Monksmoor Farm near Daventry. The huntsman, Lord Chesham, was further honoured by a second monument midway between Pitsford and Brixworth, said to have been paid for by the people of both villages in gratitude for the charitable work he had undertaken on their behalf. Sadly now defaced, it once read: 'Erected by friends in the Pytchley country. To the memory of Charles Compton W. 3rd Baron Chesham, KCB, who met his death whilst hunting with the Pytchley hounds. November 9th, 1907. Aged 56. A good man, a gallant soldier, a true Sportman.'

Places of Interest in the Neighbourhood
   6. The Ruin on the Green (Boughton Green)
   7. An Unwelcome Obelisk (Boughton)
   8. The Castellated Follies of Boughton
23. Famous American Ancestry in Northamptonshire (Ecton)
46. Scratch Dials (Ecton)

The battle monument on the wrong site in Naseby.

37 'To Commemorate that Great and Decisive Battle.'

Position: Naseby.
OS Map: Kettering & Corby, Sheet 141.
Map Ref: SP694784 and SP684799.
Access: Naseby stands on the B4036 between Clipston and Cold Ashby. The earlier monument is to the north of the village by the roadside, whilst the later is 1 mile north-west on the road to Sibbertoft.

Naseby is undoubtedly most famous for the Civil War battle fought here between the Parliamentarians and Royalists in 1645. Over 20,000 men took part, in the battle, which ended in a decisive victory for Fairfax and Cromwell.

Incredibly, the significance of the battle was not recognized, nor those who died commemorated, until an obelisk was built almost 180 years later. Approximately sixty feet tall, it was built on an artificial stone mound, and surmounted with a pyramidal capping. Hence, from it's styling alone, the monument might be considered a folly, for what has an Egyptian 'needle' to do with this piece of English history? In addition, the inscription inaccurately describes the field in which it stands as that in which the battle took place.

Proposals for a second monument on the correct site were soon put forward, and the monument finally built in 1936 one mile north of the village. More recent accounts of the battle have suggested that it too is positioned inaccurately by some five hundred yards, as the inscription claims that it marks the spot from where Cromwell led his charge: there are no plans to move it.

Local tradition claims that in accordance with Cromwell's dying wish, his body was smuggled out of London for secret burial nine feet beneath the surface of the Naseby battlefield.

Places of Interest in the Neighbourhood
3. The Copper Ball and Iron Jug (Naseby)
9. History in the Making (Kelmarsh)
9. The Garden Gnome of the Stately Home (Lamport)

The 'Source of the Avon' spout within the shrubbery of Manor Farm.

38 The Copper Ball and Iron Jug

Position: Naseby.
OS Map: Kettering & Corby, Sheet 141.
Map Ref: SP689781.
Access: Naseby stands on the B4036 between Clipston and Cold Ashby.

At the Church of All Saints in the centre of Naseby, and opposite, in the grounds of Manor Farm, are two local curiosities. The first is a large copper ball, known locally as 'Naseby Old Man', which was brought to England by Sir Giles Allington shortly after Henry VIII raided Boulogne in 1544. Sir Giles used it for decorative purposes at his house in Cambridgeshire until the house was dismantled. The ball was purchased by a Naseby resident, who, in 1790, also paid for a timber frame to be erected upon the then incomplete church spire. This was suitably clad and capped with the upturned copper ball, to which was fixed ornamental ironwork and a weather-vane. It stood for seventy years or so, until in 1859 the church was restored. The makeshift spire was replaced by one of stone and the copper ball presented to it's pur-chaser's descendants at the Hall. After some years in a topiary garden at Maidwell Hall, the much travelled copper ball was returned to the church – where it is now displayed.

The second curiosity sits within a shrubbery in front of Manor Farm, and is clearly visible over the wall from the footpath. In a roughly circular depression, stands a large conical iron jug. Beneath the collar and spout at the top is written, in raised lettering: 'Source of the Avon, 822.'

Places of Interest in the Neighbourhood
7. 'To Commemorate that Great and Decisive Battle (Naseby)
9. History in the Making (Kelmarsh)
0. The Garden Gnome at the Stately Home (Lamport)

39 History in the Making

Position: Kelmarsh.
OS Map: Kettering & Corby, Sheet 141.
Map Ref: SP737792.
Access: 8 miles west of Kettering and 4½ miles south of Market Harborough, Kelmarsh stands on the A508 road from Northampton.

During the 1960s an original drawing of 1778 was discovered for a pair of entrance lodges and gates, intended for Kelmarsh Hall, but not built. It is to the Hall's benefit, and the county's, that following the discovery, a decision was taken to implement the design. Modern requirements called for some refinement of the original drawing, but the south lodges which today front onto the village crossroads are largely as the designer intended, almost two centuries earlier.

Places of Interest in the Neighbourhood
37. 'To Commemorate that Great and Decisive Battle' (Naseby)
38. The Copper Ball and Iron Jug (Naseby)
40. The Garden Gnome at the Stately Home (Lamport)
41. The Deserted Village of Faxton

The entrance lodges to Kelmarsh Hall.

40. The Garden Gnome at the Stately Home

Position: Lamport.
OS Map: Kettering & Corby, Sheet 141.
Map Ref: SP760745 and SP760748.
Access: 2 ½ miles north of Brixworth and 5 ½ miles south-west of Rothwell, Lamport lies on the A508 and B576, with access to the Hall ¼ mile south of the junction on the Northampton road. The bakehouse is set back from the road, to the left of the B576 towards Rothwell.

The first of Lamport's curiosities dates from the 1670's. To the south-east of the Hall, standing in the centre of the lawn, is a circular stone structure. It is all that remains of a 17th century cock-fighting pit, and is one of only a few such pits in the county.

A second unusual feature of the gardens can be seen looking back towards the house. Built in 1848, what appears to be a sham ruin conceals an alpine garden with miniature rocks and caves, dwarf trees and the traces of former water features. It was further adorned in its original state by a number of garden gnomes especially imported from Germany

The last of the original garden gnomes at Lamport.

by Sir Charles Isham. As such, they were the first garden gnomes in England. Of the original 150 only one survives in a case housed in the Hall library.

Elsewhere in Lamport is a red brick building whose history is recorded on an inscribed stone above the front door. Built in 1735, it was originally a dovecote. Later converted into a bakehouse, the inscribed stone says quite simply:

> 'Where pigeons once did sport and fly
> You now may bake a pigeon pie'

Places of Interest in the Neighbourhood
36. The Pytchley's Proud Past (Pitsford, Brixworth)
39. History in the Making (Kelmarsh)
41. The Deserted Village of Faxton
42. An Ecclesiastical Rarity (Hannington)

Remnants of the church, Faxton.

41 The Deserted Village of Faxton

Position: Faxton.
OS Map: Kettering & Corby, Sheet 141.
Map Ref: SP783753.
Access: Situated about 1 mile north of Old and 1 ½ miles east of
Lamport, Faxton may be reached by taking the B576 off the A508,
followed by a right turn to the village of Old. Here, take the left turn at
the church and the left fork road out of the village. About 1 ½ miles
north stands Old Lodge with a narrow track leading down sloping
ground to the left. Walking from the low ground, through the gates and
up the narrow track opposite, an island copse of trees and shrub can be
seen to the left. In here may be found the remains.

In a lonely field, partially hidden by an unchecked growth of shrubs,
bushes and weeds, are a number of stone floor slabs and, within a
protective circle of fencing, an octagonal stone stump with a moulded
base and capital. These are the remains of the Church of St Denis
which, until recently, stood on this site and served the ever dwindling
community of Faxton village.

   In 1901 the church and eleven houses were described, while another
account of the village from the late 1920s identifies a few cottages, the
church and almshouse ruins. The church eventually fell into disrepair
and was demolished in 1958 leaving only these few remnants, with some
of its fittings transferred to churches at Kettering and Lamport, or to
the Victoria and Albert Museum.

   One house is now all that remains at Faxton, while nearby Faxton
Grange might almost be said to be in Lamport.

Places of Interest in the Neighbourhood
40. The Garden Gnome of the Stately Home (Lamport)
42. An Ecclesiastical Rarity (Hannington)
49. One Night of Madness (Broughton)

42 An Ecclesiastical Rarity

Position: Hannington.
OS Map: Kettering & Corby, Sheet 141.
Map Ref: SP812709.
Access: Approximately mid-way between Kettering and Northampton, Hannington lies 1 mile to the west of the A43, with the church at the intersection of roads from Walgrave and Holcot.

The small village of Hannington, just two miles east of the Pitsford reservoir, contains many pleasant old buildings. One in particular is worthy of note, not only on a local level, but also in the context of national history. For here is a 13th century church, the like of which is only to be found in three other places in the British Isles.

The small church of St Peter and St Paul is built with chancel, nave, tower and a north porch. In common with many small churches, there are no side aisles, but the location of two columns and a connecting arcade marching from the tower to the chancel have created a double nave, or more accurately, a bisected nave.

Other examples of this unusual internal arrangement are to be found at Gaythorpe (Lincs), Wootton Bassett (Wiltshire) and Stretford (Herefordshire), and range in dates from early 13th century to early 14th century. The occasional example may also be found on the Continent, particularly with monastic establishments combining both monks and nuns. It was once thought a similar monastic arrangement existed at Hannington, but this and other suggestions put forward to explain this architectural oddity have since been discredited.

One further unusual feature about the church is that it stands on an almost circular mound, rising five or six feet above the village street. The suggestion has been made that the elevated ground was a Moot Mound – where disputes were once settled and local laws passed in the presence of the assembled community.

43 Dolben's Disappearing Delights

Position: Finedon.
OS Map: Kettering & Corby, Sheet 141.
Map Ref: SP921721.
Access: 5 ½ miles south-east of Kettering and 3 ½ miles north-east of Wellingborough, Finedon stands at the crossing of the A6 and the A510. On the southern corner plot of land at this junction is the obelisk.

Finedon is fortunate to have had a Lord of the Manor such as Sir English Dolben, whose affection for antiquities and appreciation of his surroundings led to numerous improvements of the Finedon Hall grounds. With the help of his father, Sir William Dolben, a dam was built across the town brook forming a large lake in 1787. In the previous year, upon the instruction of Sir English, the royal connections of the village had been celebrated by the construction of Queen Edith's Cross. As wife of Edward the Confessor and sister of King Harold, England's last Saxon king, Queen Edith had been the owner of Finedon

Sir English Dolben's obelisk at Finedon.

at the time of the Norman invasion in 1066. The monument erected in her memory consisted of a stone column on a square base crowned with an iron circle of spikes.

Sadly, of all the improvements made to the Hall grounds, none survive. In 1880, an outbreak of typhoid was blamed on the lake which was drained as a result. In the 1930s, the Cross was attacked and demolished by hooligans. The fragments were collected together and re-erected in the garden of the Bell Inn, but even this has since disappeared to be replaced by the pub car-park. The grounds are now a housing estate and the other features have been razed to the ground.

Elsewhere, at the crossing of the two main roads, Sir English erected a small obelisk 'as a direction pillar and to record the many blessings of 1789'. The date may refer to the birth of his fifth daughter and his father's second marriage, but as the inscriptions have now eroded, this remains uncertain. Happily the obelisk has survived.

Places of Interest in the Neighbourhood
44. A Gothic Infatuation (Finedon)
45. The Latest Tall Storey (Finedon)
48. The Wellington Tower (Burton Latimer)

The windmill conversion of Ex-Mill Cottage in Finedon.

70

44 A Gothic Infatuation

Position: Finedon.
OS Map: Kettering & Corby, Sheet 141.
Map Ref: SP911718, SP908723 and SP914717.
Access: 5 ½ miles south-east of Kettering and 3 ½ miles north-east of
Wellingborough, Finedon stands at the crossing of the A6 and A510.
From the A6, take the Wellingborough road and turn right at the
Mulso Arms public house. Down the hill the Bell Inn is on the left.
Continuing up the hill, the Hall and ice-tower are off to the left, whilst
Ex-Mill Cottage is further along Station Road, also on the left.

In July 1885 William Mackworth married Frances Dolben, the younger
of two grand-daughters and beneficiaries of the estate of Sir English
Dolben at Finedon Hall. Mackworth took the additional surname and
arms of Dolben and, embarking upon a programme of further building
around the Hall, grounds and village, indulged his personal preference
for the Gothic style.

   The windmill constructed by his predecessor in 1818 had become
redundant, and was an irresistible target for Mr Mackworth-Dolben's
attentions. He removed the sails, cabin and internal mechanism, adding
tiered castellations, pseudo-Gothic windows and a millstone with the
letters R.E.S.T. He also added two stone shields bearing his initials, and
a stone scroll with the name EX MILL COTTAGE, although it also
became known as Windmill Cottage and Dolben's Folly. After remaining empty for a number of years, it was acquired and further modified
by the present owner.

   The Bell Inn is another example of Gothic conversion to an earlier
building. In 1872, the front facade was rebuilt, introducing the porch
and distinctive detailing, and once again recalling Finedon's royal connection with Queen Edith.

   The Hall too acquired gargoyles, emblems and simple decoration. To
its west, a four storey circular ice-house tower was constructed, while
nearby a trio of Gothic arches, a gateway arch and a grotto garden were
also created. Of these, however, all that remains is the ice-house tower,
which has successfully been incorporated into a modern house.

Places of Interest in the Neighbourhood
43. Dolben's Disappearing Delights (Finedon)
45. The Latest Tall Storey (Finedon)
48. The Wellington Tower (Burton Latimer)

45 The Latest Tall Storey

Position: Finedon.
OS Map: Kettering & Corby, Sheet 141.
Map Ref: SP926717.
Access: 5 ½ miles south-east of Kettering and 3 ½ miles north-east of Wellingborough, Finedon stands at the crossing of the A6 and A510. The tower may be seen on the left of the A6 when heading south towards Irthlingborough.

Constructed between 1903-6, Finedon's decorative water tower was designed to supply the village and a proposed swimming bath. It has a two storey entrance porch leading directly to the base of the octagonal tower, which is buttressed at each of the corners. Banded in brickwork of contrasting colours, the walls step outwards towards the top, where windows are incorporated within decorative arcading.

At the time of its construction, Finedon could boast towers to the church, Hall , ice-house, Ex-Mill cottage and one known as the Volta Tower. With such a tradition, it must have been almost obligatory to

Finedon water tower.

The now collapsed Volta Tower at Finedon.

produce a water tower able to add to the display, and the splendid Volta Tower undoubtedly inspired much of the detail.

It had castellations, arcading, crosses, a motto and date (1863) all identified in materials of contrasting colours. Above the entrance porch was the Mackworth-Dolben coat of arms, while to either side of the entrance door were the words 'VOLTA' and 'TOWER'. Named after the man-of-war on which young William Mackworth-Dolben had been serving: he was drowned while in a small boat capsized by a seal. In memory of his son, Squire Dolben ordered the construction of the tower on a site next to the cemetery.

This remarkable structure was sadly flawed, causing it to collapse in November 1951. The local newspaper of the day reported that the tower had been built without mortar to bind the great stone slabs together, and that its collapse had been preceded by the loud rumbling sound of land subsidence.

73

Scratch dial on the south porch of Ecton Church.

46 Scratch Dials

Position: Stanwick & Ecton.
OS Map: Kettering & Corby, Sheet 141.
Northampton & Milton Keynes, Sheet 152.
Map Ref: SP980714 and SP829635.
Access: 7 ½ miles south-east of Kettering, Stanwick stands between
Irthlingborough and Raunds, just off the A605. Ecton is 3 ½ miles east
of Northampton, on the A4500.

The earliest sundials divided the working day into 'tides' rather than
hours (eg. noontide, eventide etc.), or the times of the day which re-
lated to specific religious services. They were most frequently positioned
by the south doorway of churches, from where the ringing of the bell
would summon the congregation. Generally no more than six inches
across, crudely scratched lines radiating from a hole in the wall indicated the critical times from the shadow cast by a removable gnomon,
or indicator.

A handful of 'scratch-dials' survive on Northamptonshire churches,
such as at Stanwick. As they were carved in the softer building stones
of the county, many have been considerably eroded and almost lost.
Others have been more fortunate, possibly because the relevant original
stone had been cut out for re-use elsewhere, and a replacement stone
re-cut or inscribed with a new programme of critical times. Such an
example is at Ecton church, where one is marked in 24 alternating long
and short lines within a double ring, and another, suffering greater
erosion, is of a more simple arrangement.

The range of designs seems endless. They are widespread throughout
the county, and if the search for them can be frustrating their discovery
is always rewarding.

Places of Interest in the Neighbourhood
Ecton: 9. William Shakespeare's Tree (Abington Park)
  10. The Well in the Tower (Abington)
  14. Of Buildings, Beehives and Balustrades (Castle Ashby)
  23. Famous American Ancestry in Northants (Ecton)
Stanwick: 43. Dolben's Disappearing Delights (Finedon)
  44. A Gothic Infatuation (Finedon)
  45. The Latest Tall Storey (Finedon)

47 An Unexpected Find

Position: St Mary the Virgin, Woodford.
OS Map: Kettering & Corby, Sheet 141.
Map Ref: SP969767.
Access: Woodford is 2 miles south-west of Thrapston, on minor roads from the A604 to the Addingtons and Irthlingborough. The church is to the east of the village.

In the spring of 1860 a strange and unexpected discovery was made in the church of St Mary the Virgin, Woodford, during some much needed restoration in the north aisle. One of the stone arches in the colonnade had been propped so that the adjacent arcade column could be repaired. Removal of the prop revealed that the stone it had been supporting had shattered. The workmen carefully removed the broken pieces, revealing a hollow compartment and what was thought to be a bird's nest. In fact it was a small round box, inside which was a cloth ball containing a human heart, black with age but well preserved. Arrangements were made for the remains to be placed in a case and fitted within the recess from whence it came, where it may still be seen today.

Recent research has identified two local names that could perhaps lay claim to the heart: Roger de Kirkton, who died and was buried in Norfolk, or Sir Walter Trayli, who died whilst on Crusade and was buried abroad in 1290. The effigies of Sir Walter and his wife are to be found at the top of the north aisle.

One further theory speculates that it is the heart of a pre-Reformation vicar who fled abroad taking with him a valuable chalice. His successor is said to have later found his body and the chalice, returning with the heart as proof to the parishioners that he was now dead.

As to why the heart should be concealed within the structure of the church remains unclear, but a secret burial may support the latter theory.

Places of Interest in the Neighbourhood
29. Toll Houses of Old England (Twywell and Sudborough)
48. The Wellington Tower (Burton Latimer)

48 The Wellington Tower

Position: On the A510 north of Finedon.
OS Map: Kettering & Corby, Sheet 141.
Map Ref: SP935749.
Access: The Wellington Tower stands by the old Finedon to Thrapston road, 2 miles from the Addingtons, 2 miles from Burton Latimer, 2 miles from Cranford and 2 miles from Finedon. Thanks to an 'S' bend in the Parish boundary, it lies in the Parish of Burton Latimer and is also known as 'Burton Round House'.

Construction of the Round House may have started in 1813 when modifications to Woodford House were underway for the estate's new owner, General Charles Arbuthnot. The General was apparently a great friend of the Duke of Wellington, who frequently stayed at Woodford. It was on one such visit that the Duke remarked how the

The Wellington Tower on the Burton Latimer parish boundary.

terrain of the area reminded him of the Waterloo battlefield. Shortly afterwards, the tower's construction was completed incorporating a plaque and the wording: 'PANORAMA. WATERLOO VICTORY. JUNE 18 AD 1825'. From the second floor a short flight of steps led to a turret from which to survey the surrounding countryside.

By the mid-19th century, the Round House was a wayside inn. Because of its popularity and remote location, the 70 acre field opposite was frequently used for brawling and dog racing. Eventually, the inn became the private 'Waterloo Victory Social Club' which, in 1895, moved to Finedon and became known as the 'Pam' (derived from the panorama wording on the Round House plaque). In turn, the Round House became home to a farmer whose 130 acres were distributed over four parishes. It was said he would breakfast in Burton Latimer, leave his house and step into Great Addington, climb a fence into Woodford and work the land in the Parish of Finedon!

Places of Interest in the Neighbourhood

49 One Night of Madness

Position: Broughton.
OS Map: Kettering & Corby, Sheet 141.
Map Ref: SP835758.
Access: 2½ miles south-west of Kettering, Broughton is now by-passed by the A43, but signposted from it.

On the first Sunday after December 12th each year the inhabitants of Broughton enact the bizarre tradition of 'Broughton Feast Sunday'. The traditional events call for participants to congregate in the last minutes of Saturday night immediately outside the rectory gates to await the last stroke of midnight. With everywhere else in near silence, the final chime signifies the commencement of an unmusical percussive din, created by the beating of metal cans. At this point the gathering parades around the lonely streets of Broughton, awakening the villagers and reminding them that the great day has arrived. When the participants feel they have adequately honoured tradition the impromptu band disperses to await the next year's revelry.

The origins of this strange event are not recorded but have produced a number of theories. Could it symbolise the despatch of undesirables, either of this world or the next? As the church is dedicated to St Andrew, could it be a belated celebration of St Andrew's Day, or does it record some far more mundane event in the history of the village?

One thing is for certain, it has survived the Parish Council's attempts to stop it in 1929 and the Second World War, when a lone individual kept the tradition alive. The ceremony has not been neglected since its inception as failure to perform it, even for just one year, would signify the end of the custom.

Places of Interest in the Neighbourhood
1. The Deserted Village of Faxton
2. An Ecclesiastical Rarity (Hannington)

50 The Fading Sundial

Position: Weekley.
OS Map: Kettering & Corby, Sheet 141.
Map Ref: SP889809.
Access: Weekley stands 1 mile north-east of Kettering on the A43, with the Hospital building close to the church.

During the early years of Queen Victoria's reign it is reported that while on a visit to the county, the queen stopped the carriage in Weekley to ask of its name. It is easy to understand why, for the village is still largely unspoilt, and retains the charm that made it so attractive to her.

Venturing from the main road towards the church, further questions might have been asked of the curious porch to be seen on one of the buildings there. The solid wooden door is flanked at its head by stone corbelling supporting a canopy with, at either end, tall pointed obelisks supported on shells. The face of the building bears a coat of arms and the date 1611. Shortly before the queen's visit, a large and colourful sundial had been painted above the coat of arms with the motto 'Tempora Labuntur Tacitisque Senescimus' (time flows by and we grow old with the silent years). The splendid paintwork, now sadly much faded, includes the date 1831, while further obelisks appear at roof level.

The building was the Weekley Hospital, erected in accordance with laws passed during Queen Elizabeth's reign, to provide 'hospitals, bidings or working houses for the poor'. The arms over the door are those of the Montagues of Boughton House, and it was they who eventually purchased the building back from the Charity Commissioners and converted it into the impressive single residence that can be seen today.

Places of Interest in the Neighbourhood
13. The Queen Eleanor Crosses (Geddington)
51. Portable Curiosities at Boughton House (Weekley)
68. Monument to the Holy Trinity (Rushton)
69. The Largest Dovecote in the British Isles (Newton)

he splendid entrance to the former hospital building at Weekley.

51 Portable Curiosities at Boughton House

Position: Weekley.
OS Map: Kettering & Corby, Sheet 141.
Map Ref: SP900815.
Access: 1½ miles north-east of Kettering, Boughton House and Park lies east off the A43 with access from the road between Geddington and Grafton Underwood. The House opens to the public during the summer months.

Boughton House combines a 16th century complex of buildings with a rare example of French Renaissance architecture as its north facade. It is also said to have 7 courtyards, 12 entrances, 52 chimney stacks and 365 windows.

Exhibited in an unfinished wing of the house is another rarity: a portable Chinese tent. Made in the late 18th century for the grounds of Montagu House in Whitehall, this twelve sided structure has a rigid timber frame on a raised base and walls which pivot outwards to form a canopy roof. Above each of the 12 posts, curved rafters gently sweep up to a crowning ring and ball, complete with roaring dragon. Inside, the oilskin roof is brightly decorated in red on a yellow background with further contorting dragons. It may be the only existing example of its type in England.

Another exhibit is a model bridge made for the 2nd Duke of Montagu. Fortunately the proposed bridge, which was flamboyantly Gothic with three arches and a pinnacled roof at its centre, was never built. Its proposed setting in the open countryside in front of the impressive north facade of the House was totally unsympathetic to its surroundings. As a model however, it is both a minor curiosity and a rare survival, for few such models remain.

Places of Interest in the Neighbourhood
13. The Queen Eleanor Crosses (Geddington)
50. The Fading Sundial (Weekley)
68. Monument to the Holy Trinity (Rushton)
69. The Largest Dovecote in the British Isles (Newton)

52 'Bocase Stone' Theories

Position: Harry's Park Wood.
OS Map: Kettering & Corby, Sheet 141.
Map Ref: SP948875.
Access: 4 miles east of Corby and 1 mile north of Brigstock, travel east from Stanion on the A6116 past the turn to the right for Brigstock and take the first no-through road on the left. Walk the bridleway for about ½ mile, past the buildings on the right, to where two gates cross the track. The gate on the left leads to an overgrown lane and, within 20 yards or so, the Bocase Stone.

The Bocase Stone is roughly three feet high and eighteen inches wide. It leans slightly and bears two curious inscriptions: 'In this place grew the Bocase Tree', and less prominently 'Here grew the Bocase Tree' (the latter is almost buried in the ground). It is said that the mysterious stone was erected in the 17th century, shortly after the tree was felled.

As the stone lies deep in the heart of the ancient Rockingham Forest it has been suggested that a member of the royal family killed a stag or buck somewhere nearby, which in turn was skinned, or 'cased': hence 'buck-case tree'. Alternatively, it may mark the spot where announcements connected to forest rights were made, as indicated by the Saxon word for such a place: 'bocas'.

A third and equally plausible explanation might be that the tree marked the spot where the King's men met to practice their skills with the longbow. There is a long, narrow field nearby, formerly referred to as 'the bowcast', which may have been the site of the local butts.

The final theory inevitably concerns English folklore's most popular hero, Robin Hood. It is said he hid his longbow in a recess of the tree in order to escape from the guards of Sir Ralph de Manville after being ambushed at Brigstock church. From this, the term 'bocase' can be seen to derive from 'bow-case'.

Places of Interest in the Neighbourhood
3. The Gargoyle Well(Fermyn Woods Hall)
4. An Unfinished Masterpiece (Lyveden)
2. Bone of Contention (Stanion)

53 The Gargoyle Well

Position: Fermyn Woods Hall.
OS Map: Kettering & Corby, Sheet 141.
Map Ref: SP959871.
Access: 4½ miles east of Corby and 1½ miles north of Brigstock,
Fermyn Woods Hall stands on the minor road from Brigstock to Lower
Benefield. Take the left turn off the A427 in Lower Benefield and the
Hall is about 2½ miles on the right.

To the west of Fermyn Woods Hall stands a fifteen feet high six-sided
stone column. Its frieze incorporates carved gargoyles that look as if
they are about to leap to the ground. On one side is an iron turning
handle, whilst opposite is the head and neck of an open-mouthed beast.
For the column marks a well, whose waters were once pumped into the
large stone trough at its base.

  It formerly bore the initials A.G. and F.P., for Anne and Gertrude
FitzPatrick, and a date of 1829, which matches their many alterations
to the Hall.

Places of Interest in the Neighbourhood
52. 'Bocase Stone' Theories (Brigstock)
54. An Unfinished Masterpiece (Lyveden)
62. Bone of Contention (Stanion)

The well-head in the grounds of Fermyn Woods Hall.

54 An Unfinished Masterpiece

Position: Lyveden.
OS Map: Kettering & Corby, Sheet 141.
Map Ref: SP984854.
Access: 2 miles east of Brigstock and 4 miles south-west of Oundle, Lyveden New Beild stands in open land about ½ mile south of the minor road known as the Harley Way.

Approximately ten miles separate two of England's most notable monuments to the turbulent years of religious upheaval which followed the Act of Supremacy in 1534. They date from the final years of the 16th century, and display an ingenious use of mathematics and Catholic symbolism. Both were the work of one man, Sir Thomas Tresham, Lord of the Manors of Lyveden and Rushton (see No 68).

In 1581 Sir Thomas began a twelve year period of imprisonment for 'harbouring priests'. Upon his release, he began work at Lyveden. In a development from his earlier building at Rothwell (see No 67), Tresham's first demonstration of faith, the 'New Beild', took religious themes. Inscriptions and emblems were used to illustrate their significance in a numerical format based upon three, five, seven and nine. Of three floors and cruciform in plan, each arm of the cross is square with a bay window on the end wall. These bays each have five sides of five feet in length. Each wing has a perimeter of 81 feet (9 x 9

The incomplete 'New Beild' at Lyveden.

feet). As each arm of the cross is an equal square, they enclose a fifth square at the centre. Above the ground floor windows is a symbolic frieze of seven religious emblems, whilst to the upper frieze are inscribed quotations from the Latin Bible.

Sir Thomas was re-imprisoned in 1600 and died in 1605. The New Beild was never completed, but its remains are cared for by the National Trust and stand in picturesque solitude as evidence of one man's willingness to die for his faith.

Places of Interest in the Neighbourhood
52. 'Bocase Stone' Theories (Brigstock)
53. The Gargoyle Well (Fermyn Woods Hall)
55. The Old Watch House (Pilton)

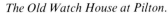

The Old Watch House at Pilton.

55 The Old Watch House

Position: Pilton.
OS Map: Kettering & Corby, Sheet 141.
Map Ref: TL022845.
Access: Pilton is 2½ miles south-west of Oundle and 3½ miles north-east of Thrapston on a minor road just off the A605.

The tiny village of Pilton comprises a handful of small houses arranged along a single lane, with a former Manor House of the Treshams and the Church of St Mary's and All Saints sitting together in a meadow. On the corner at the far end of the lane, just before the first gates into the meadow, is a three storey stone building, known as the 'Bede House', or alternatively the 'Old Watch House'.

The ground and first floors present nothing significantly unusual, but on reaching the second floor the builder must have experienced a change of heart. Here the windows are flanked by vertical shafts rising from miniature heads carved in stone. Rising from the ridge of the north gable is a brick shaft embellished with decorative stonework and a stepped brick pyramid capping. On each face of the shaft is a pair of short but narrow openings, while at the roof line may be seen an arched window with a stone lintel.

One local tale inevitably links the Treshams of Pilton with those of Lyveden, three miles to the west, and stories of secret Recusant meetings. It is said that the shaft acted as a lookout, providing advance warning of approaching soldiers and it is from this source that the building has the name of 'Old Watch House'. Another local account maintains that the shaft was a chimney whose smoke seeped through the side vents. Referred to in 1515 as a new house, documents testify to its construction as a three function building of Bede House and grain store with curate's living quarters above. A simple modification, however, could have created the 'lookout' at a later date.

Places of Interest in the Neighbourhood
54. An Unfinished Masterpiece (Lyveden)
56. Re-erected Church Fragments (Achurch)
57. A Masonic Plaque (Aldwinkle)

56 Re-erected Church Fragments

Position: Achurch.
OS Map: Kettering & Corby, Sheet 141.
Map Ref: TL022833 and TL023828.
Access: 3 ½ miles south of Oundle, 3 ½ miles north-east of Thrapston
and 8 ½ miles south-east of Corby, Achurch stands on the minor road
between Thorpe Waterville and Lilford Park near the A605. The church
is at the end of the village lane while the well is by the village road.

In the late 18th century, Sir Thomas Powys, first Lord Lilford, obtained
an Act of Parliament authorising the demolition of Lilford church: the
salvaged materials to be used for repairing the nearby Church of
St John the Baptist, Achurch. The surplus stone was used to build
a picturesque landscape feature in the form of three arches in the
wooded area known as 'The Lynches', due north of the church tower at
Achurch. To one side of a slow running stream by the River Nene,
stands one of the three arches, whilst the many fallen stones indicate the
fate of the other two.

A second curiosity at Achurch is the picturesque well-head in the
village erected by the 4th Lord Lilford in memory of his eldest son,
Thomas Alberton Powys, who died in 1882.

Places of Interest in the Neighbourhood
55. The Old Watch House (Pilton)
57. A Masonic Plaque (Aldwinkle)

The re-erected remains of Lilford Church, Achurch

57 A Masonic Plaque

Position: Aldwinkle.
OS Map: Kettering & Corby, Sheet 141.
Map Ref: TL007817.
Access: 2 miles north of Thrapston, Aldwinkle may be reached via the
A605, heading west from Thorpe Waterville. Lowick Lane is the first on
the left in the village.

To the south-west of All Saints Church in the narrow and winding
Lowick Lane, stands Tavern Cottage. On the east elevation facing the
lane is a plaque bearing castellated towers, mason's tools and a Latin
inscription. The initials 'J.A.' remain a mystery, but the remainder
translates as 'Believers in Christ have eternal life'. The plaque is not
original to the building, having been transferred in 1954 from a row of
cottages in nearby Titchmarsh at the time of their demolition.

Places of Interest in the Neighbourhood
29. Toll Houses of Old England (Sudborough)
55. The Old Watch House (Pilton)
56. Re-erected Church Fragments (Achurch)

The masonic plaque on Tavern Cottage, Aldwinkle.

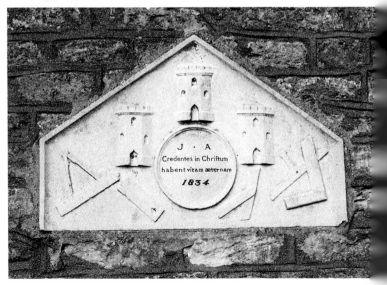

58 Nutty World Championships

Position: Ashton.
OS Map: Peterborough, Sheet 142.
Map Ref: TL055883.
Access: The village of Ashton is 1 mile east of Oundle, just off the A605.

For all but one day of the year Ashton is a picturesque village of thatched stone cottages nestling engagingly around the Green. But on the second Sunday of October this peaceful setting is shattered by the arrival of thousands of spectators to watch Northamptonshire's nuttiest sporting contest – the World Conker Championships.

As with many traditional events, the championships have developed from modest beginnings. In 1965, a number of 'would-be' anglers were deterred from fishing by bad weather. Meeting in the local pub, they decided that a game of conkers would make an ideal substitute. In subsequent years the event was repeated, attracting a small following and requiring a degree of organisation and control. The rules of the competition have remained roughly unchanged since the first tournament, although separate competitions for women and children have since been introduced. The addition of other games and craft stalls, together with the wearing of fancy dress costumes by participants and spectators alike has in turn added to the atmosphere.

In 1990 to mark the championship's Silver Jubilee, 25 young horse chestnut trees were planted in order that future generations might have an ample supply of conkers with which to do battle, simultaneously maintaining a tradition which continues to raise thousands of pounds for charity.

Places of Interest in the Neighbourhood
55. The Old Watch House (Pilton)
56. Re-erected Church Fragments (Achurch)
59. The Fotheringhay Legacy (Fotheringhay)

59 The Fotheringhay Legacy

Position: Fotheringhay.
OS Map: Peterborough, Sheet 142.
Map Ref: TL061930.
Access: 3 ½ miles north-east of Oundle and 8 ½ miles south-west of Peterborough, Fotheringhay is signposted from the A605 through the village of Tansor. Crossing the bridge into Fotheringhay, the road turns to the left where the Castle site is to the right, down a narrow track between farm buildings and open farmland.

The cursed and ill-fated castle of Fotheringhay has almost completely vanished from its site by the River Nene. Only a modest mass of stone, the moat and the earthworks of the great mound remain. Gone too, are all illustrations of the fortress, but perhaps this is how it was meant to be. For while the castle stood, its owners and custodians seemed fated with misfortune, ill-health or violent death.

Most famous for the execution of Mary Queen of Scots, the castle's demolition began within 40 years of her death. The banqueting hall and other portions of the castle were used in the construction of Conington Castle, Huntingdonshire, where its new owner Sir Robert Bruce Cotton promptly died upon its completion!

Other fragments went to Fineshade Abbey, the Talbot Inn at Oundle (where the staircase is said to be haunted by Queen Mary's ghost), Kings Cliffe and elsewhere. Scottish thistles now grow over the site of the castle and are affectionately known as Queen Mary's Tears.

Just a few years before the final destruction of the castle in 1863, the self-appointed guide to the site, Robert Wyatt, made an amazing discovery. Buried within rubbish, he stumbled upon Queen Mary's signet ring, given to her by her second husband, Lord Darnley. It bears their monogram bound up in a lover's knot, and, within the hoop, a lion and crowned shield with the inscription: 'Henri L. Darnley 1565'. The ring was presented to the British Museum, where it is exhibited.

Places of Interest in the Neighbourhood
58. Nutty World Championships (Ashton)
72. The Solitary Statue (Blatherwyke)
73. 'Heels over Head' Burial (Blatherwyke)
80. The Bishop's Sundial (Upton)

60 A Lighthouse in the Forest

Position: Weldon.
OS Map: Kettering & Corby, Sheet 141.
Map Ref: SP928893.
Access: 2 miles east of Corby, Weldon lies on the A427 from Oundle, and to the east of the A43 from Kettering. The two routes are connected by two minor roads through the village, the church stands on the land between them.

Local folklore tells the story of how the church at Weldon-in-the-Woods came by its most prominent feature. A traveller apparently became lost in Rockingham Forest. Finding himself on sloping ground, he climbed to the highest point, from where, above the tree tops, he

The church at Weldon-in-the-Woods.

could see the church. With this as a guide, he made his way to a path which led to the village. As a thanks offering, he later financed the building of a guiding lantern light at the top of the tower.

The present domed lantern surmounted by its splendid iron weathercock maintains the tradition by housing lighted candles on every New Year's Eve, so that it becomes an unusual inland lighthouse.

Places of Interest in the Neighbourhood
61. The Village Roundhouse (Weldon)
62. Bone of Contention (Stanion)
63. The Curious Custom of the 'Pole Fair' (Corby)
70. Ancient Advertisements (Weldon, Gretton)

Weldon's lock-up on the green.

61 The Village Roundhouse

Position: Weldon.
OS Map: Kettering & Corby, Sheet 141.
Map Ref: SP928894.
Access: Weldon is 2 miles east of Corby on the A427 from Oundle, and to the east of the A43 from Kettering. Follow the A427 through the village: the Roundhouse may be seen by the side of the road.

At the centre of the village, standing by the old village school on the Green, is an 18th century windowless building with a conical roof surmounted by a stone orb. Its single entrance door provides access to the meagre accommodation within, which was ideally suited to its function as an overnight jail for local troublemakers.

During the 18th and early 19th centuries many villages possessed such a lock-up, be they round, square or rectangular. At Rothwell, the stairwell of the incomplete Market House (see No 67) acted as a jail, whilst at Alderton there is a cottage with a semi-circular end wall still known as 'The Roundhouse'. Such buildings frequently stood alongside the whipping post and stocks on a village Green; the traditional site for local punishments. A number of Northants villages retain and display such equipment, most notably at Aynho, Gretton and Apethorpe.

Places of Interest in the Neighbourhood
50. A lighthouse in the Forest (Weldon)
52. Bone of Contention (Stanion)
53. The Curious Custom of the 'Pole Fair' (Corby)
70. Ancient Advertisements (Weldon, Gretton)

62 Bone of Contention

Position: St Peter's Church, Stanion.
OS Map: Kettering & Corby, Sheet 141.
Map Ref: SP915868.
Access: About 1 ½ miles south-east of Corby, Stanion stands at the junction of the A43 from Kettering and the A6116 from Thrapston. The church is in the centre of the village.

Sometime during the 15th or 16th century a strange wall painting of a stag and unicorn kneeling in prayer was painted in the interior of Stanion Church. An even greater oddity on display is an enormous bone, measuring up to six feet in length. Its history has become rather vague as the Diocesan Records Office retains no account of it being installed. If its graffiti is authentic it has been an object of curiosity since the 17th century. Two versions of its origins have been put forward, one based in folklore, the other with a hint of authenticity.

Known locally as The Dun Cow's Rib, the tale is told of how a Stanion farmer owned an unnaturally large cow whose milk yield was so plentiful the entire village could be supplied from a single milking. Envious of the magical ability made famous by the claim, a witch from a neighbouring hamlet set about the task of stopping the cow's milk. One morning, before the villagers woke, she began milking it into a sieve, reminding the animal of the claim and urging greater effort in order to fill the container. The Dun Cow produced gallon after gallon in her attempt, but as all the milk passed straight through the sieve, she was doomed to failure. Eventually, she died of exhaustion and the witch was satisfied. The rib was salvaged from the carcass by the villagers and placed in the church as a mark of respect for the cow's largesse.

The alternative version claims it to be one of a pair of whalebones brought to the village for use as a decorative entrance. But if so used, where is the second bone now, and why should the remaining bone be displayed in the church?

Places of Interest in the Neighbourhood

63. The Curious Custom of the 'Pole Fair'

Position: Corby.
OS Map: Kettering & Corby, Sheet 141.
Map Ref: SP885894.
Access: 18 miles north-east of Northampton, 12 miles south-west of Stamford. Corby village has become Corby New Town and stands on the A427 east of the A6003.

The 'Pole Fair' celebrations occur at Whitsuntide once every 20 years. Whilst no written account of it exists prior to 1862 it is thought to have originated with the Corby Charter granted by Queen Elizabeth I. The Charter constitutes a significant part of the Pole Fair custom, as it is read to the public by the Rector of Corby at dawn on the appropriate Whit-Monday. It does not, however, require or suggest the bizarre behaviour that follows. Pairs of Corby men, armed with a long pole, 'catch' unsuspecting males by stealthily approaching from the rear and thrusting the pole between the victim's legs. The pole is then hoisted shoulder-high with the 'prisoner' struggling to maintain his balance, whilst his captors make off with him to the nearest stocks.

A further aspect of the fair was the construction of ceremonial arches across all roads in and out of Corby, each incorporating a toll gate, thereby ensuring that all visitors paid for the pleasure of the undignified ride. In 1902, a variation of the custom allowed women to be 'captured', although their ceremonial ride to the stocks was a little more sedate, in a chair lashed to two poles. More recently, ceremonial ribbons have replaced the toll gates into the town. But the tradition continues, and is next due to take place in 2002.

Places of Interest in the Neighbourhood

64 In Search of Charles Dickens

Position: Rockingham and Towcester.
OS Map: Kettering & Corby, Sheet 141.
Northampton & Milton Keynes, Sheet 152.
Map Ref: SP867914 and SP692489.
Access: 1 mile north of Corby, on the A6003, Rockingham Castle is open to the public on certain days from Easter to September. Towcester is south-west of Northampton at the crossing of the A5 and A43.

Rockingham Castle, in continuous occupation by the descendants of the Watson family since 1530, frequently accommodated Charles Dickens as a guest, who with his wife, had become great friends of the family whilst holidaying in Lusanne. Dickens wrote and produced short plays at the Castle for performance in the Long Gallery. *David Copperfield* is reputed to have been largely written while staying at Rockingham.

In Towcester, the old coaching inn called 'The Saracen's Head' provided part of the inspiration for the *Pickwick Papers*, and even today retains its long stone frontage and arched entrance.

Places of Interest in the Neighbourhood
Towcester: 20. To the Memory of 'Pug' (Easton Neston)
   17. England's Largest Navigable Canal Tunnel (Blisworth)
   18. The Stoke Park Pavilions (Stoke Bruerne)
Rockingham: 63. The Curious Custom of the 'Pole Fair' (Corby)
   70. Ancient Advertisements (Weldon, Gretton)

The Saracen's Head Hotel in Towcester.

65 Statements of Defiance

Position: Dingley.
OS Map: Kettering & Corby, Sheet 141.
Map Ref: SP771877.
Access: Dingley lies on the A427, 2 miles east of Market Harborough and 7 miles west of Corby. The gatepiers of the drive leading to the Hall and church are on the left as you approach the village from Market Harborough.

Just past the Church of All Saints in the grounds of Dingley Hall stands an octagonal stone gazebo on gently sloping ground. The unusual and decorative form of the parapet is taken from the earlier parts of the Hall, and it is conceivable that the gazebo was assembled from fragments when the Hall was partly destroyed in the late 17th century.
The remaining south gateway is flanked by octagonal turrets similarly 'crowned' with circular castellations, while the text around the head of the gates prompts the question as to why, during the second year of the reign of Elizabeth I, an inscription should conclude with 'God Save the King. 1560.'?
  The Hall at that time was owned by Edward Griffin, who had been Attorney General to both Edward VI and Mary Tudor, but was not asked to continue in office by Elizabeth in 1558. Furthermore, his wife was probably a strong supporter of the 'old religion' and Griffin himself may have had Catholic sympathies. If that is the case, the king referred to was most probably Philip of Spain, indicating a wish by Griffin to see Philip's accession to the English throne and the reinstatement of Roman Catholicism. Immediately above the gateway is yet another inscription, which unfortunately had been made incomplete by the insertion of a stone pinnacle through its centre. Clearly visible is: 'What thynge of.....re but time wilepaye'. It has been suggested that the missing letters may have spelt the Elizabethan equivalent of 'dare', which in turn may be read as a reference to Henry VIII's Act of Supremacy.

Places of Interest in the Neighbourhood
66. The Lost Crypt (Rothwell)
67. In the Name of 'Friendship' (Rothwell)
68. Monument to the Holy Trinity (Rushton)

The 'crowned' gazebo of Dingley Ha

66 The Lost Crypt

Position: Holy Trinity Church, Rothwell.
OS Map: Kettering & Corby, Sheet 141.
Map Ref: SP816812.
Access: 3½ miles north-west of Kettering and 6 miles south-west of
Corby, Rothwell stands on the A6 between Kettering and Desborough.
The church crypt is open to the public on Sunday afternoons.

The parish church in Rothwell can quite legitimately boast a remarkable curiosity. During the first year of the 18th century workmen raised
a floor slab in the south aisle and discovered the vaulted roof of a 13th
century crypt or charnel house. Further investigation revealed a two-
bayed room of about thirty by fifteen feet. At the far end was the
feint outline of a fresco depicting the Resurrection. More dramatically,
the small room contained the human remains of approximately 1,500
people.
   During the following years it was suggested that the remains were
those of Danish invaders, the dead from the Battle of Naseby, or vic-
tims of the Black Death, but it is now believed that some of the remains
were originally laid in open graves round of the church and merely
moved to the crypt when the building was extended. Further burials
within the crypt probably continued until the late 16th century when the
construction of the nearby Jesus Hospital in 1591 provided sufficient
disinterred remains to fill the room. It is probably then that the crypt
was closed, and subsequently forgotten.
   Most of the remains are skulls and thigh bones which, according to
medieval belief, were those necessary if the dead were to be resurrected.
Sadly, the fresco depicting the Resurrection has all but disappeared,
and even the bones are steadily deteriorating. Only one other such collection exists in the country, at Hythe in Kent.

Places of Interest in the Neighbourhood
67. In the Name of 'Friendship' (Rothwell)
68. Monument to the Holy Trinity (Rushton)

67 In the Name of 'Friendship'

Position: Rothwell.
O.S.Map: Kettering & Corby. Sheet 141.
Map Ref: SP816813.
Access: 3 miles north-west of Kettering and 6 miles south-west of Corby, Rothwell stands on the A6 between Kettering and Desborough. Take the signposted road in the centre towards Rushton, and the Square and Market House are on the right.

Thomas Tresham was only fifteen when in 1560 he inherited the family estates from his grandfather, and thirty when he was knighted by Elizabeth I. It was thus as Sir Thomas that in 1578 his short but significant contribution to the buildings of the county began.

   Presented as a gift to the townspeople of Rothwell, his first building, The Market House, bears the undeniable stamp of geometric proportion and decorative symbolism for which Sir Thomas has become well known. In its design he developed the idea of dedicating a secular build-

Sir Thomas Tresham's market house in Rothwell.

ing to a theme, much as churches have been dedicated to saints. By means of inscriptions and decorations the Market House testifies that it was for the honour of his friends, whom he identified through the arms of ninety Northamptonshire families placed on shields round the roof parapet. This theme of friendship was further defined by inscriptions acknowledging his affection for Rothwell, Northamptonshire and the country of his birth.

The emblem of the Treshams, the trefoil, together with rectangular and oval studwork, decorate the ground floor, which was built as an open arcade with an enclosed staircase to the room above.

While construction proceeded, Tresham took up the Catholic faith, which in turn led to his imprisonment in 1581 for harbouring priests. For a while the work continued, but on Tresham's return to Northamptonshire following his release in 1593 his Catholicism diverted his attentions elsewhere (see No's 54 and 68), leaving the Market House incomplete for over three hundred years. It was finally finished in 1895, and is now used by the Local Authority.

Places of Interest in the Neighbourhood
66. The Lost Crypt (Rothwell)
68. Monument to the Holy Trinity (Rushton)

The Triangular Lodge at Rushton.

68 Monument To The Holy Trinity

Position: Rushton.
OS Map: Kettering & Corby, Sheet 141.
Map Ref: SP830830.
Access: 3 miles north-west of Kettering and 4 miles south-west of
Corby, Rushton stands at the junction of minor roads between the
A6003 and A6. The Triangular Lodge is to the west of the village,
behind high stone walls at the side of the road from Desborough. It is in
the care of English Heritage and opens to the public from April to
September.

The Triangular Lodge inside the grounds of Rushton Hall is undoubtedly the most curious building of its period, but also Sir Thomas
Tresham's most successful demonstration of his Catholic faith. During
his twelve years imprisonment from 1581, he had resolved to construct
a building which would symbolize the Holy Trinity and found that his
family name, initials, emblem and coat of arms all leant themselves to
this cause. The first syllable of his name, Tres, equates with 3: his
initials, T.T., were each in the form of the ancient 'Tau' cross; the family
emblem of a trefoil relates to Saint Patrick's emblem of the Trinity,
whilst his coat of arms displayed triangles and trefoils. Everything in
the Lodge was therefore to relate to the number three.
   There are 3 sides, each 33 feet 3 inches long, each with 3 rows of 3
windows, each with 3 triangular gables, each with an inscription running the complete length of the side with 33 letters. One of the 3 sides
faces due north and consequently, the opposite 60 degree angle points
due south. Each face of the lodge represents one of the Trinity, while
the chimney depicts the Mass.
   The chimney's method of support in the centre of the roof remained a
mystery for many years, as each of the 3 floors has no central structures, but contains a hexagonal space with triangular corner rooms, and
a single fireplace to one side on the top floor. It has been claimed that
this intentionally represents the mystery of the Mass although the large
timber beams spanning the rooms above the ceiling are now known to
provide support.
   The many inscriptions and dates which also adorn the Lodge, such as
5555, 3509 and 3098, also have religious significance in relating 1593 to
the date of creation (widely believed to be 3962 BC in the 16th century).
Appearing as it does as 15 and 93 it may also be seen as a mathametical
number in relation to the theme of 3. Each part (15 and 93) is a multiple

of 3, as is the sum of each part (6 and 12), and the sum of the whole number (18). Furthermore the date of 1593 is divisible into whole numbers by 3 no fewer than 3 times (531, 177 and 59). Can such a play with numbers be coincidental or had the ingenious Tresham calculated that 1593 (rather than 1594, its date of construction) had a divine significance to his circumstances? Whichever is the case, the Triangular Lodge should never be considered as an architectural folly, but rather as a blueprint for all that Architecture should encompass.

Places of Interest in the Neighbourhood
13. The Queen Eleanor Crosses (Geddington)
66. The Lost Crypt (Rothwell)
67. In the Name of 'Friendship' (Rothwell)
69. The Largest Dovecote in the British Isles (Newton)

The Tresham dovecote at Newton.

69 The Largest Dovecote in the British Isles

Position: Newton.
OS Map: Kettering & Corby, Sheet 141.
Map Ref: SP885834.
Access: 2½ miles north of Kettering and 3 miles south of Corby, Newton lies west of Geddington on a minor road between the A43 and A6003. The dovecote and church stand in open fields to the east of the village.

Built of limestone under a roof of Collyweston slates, this immense Elizabethan dovecote – the largest in Britain – measures approximately 54 feet by 24 feet. The walls are three feet thick in places, dividing the lofty internal space into two halves. On one side only there is a tall window, and doorway leading to each of the compartments, which contain 2,000 nesting holes. On the south elevation, just below the eaves line, an inset stone slab has the letters 'Maurice Tressham'.

During the mid 15th century the powerful Tresham family produced two lines of descendants. They built a mansion in Little Newton, depopulated the village, demolished the chapel of nearby Great Newton and adopted the one at Little Newton as a church for the personal use of the family and estate workers. Maurice Tresham, builder of the dovecote, was born in 1530, and under his guidance the family enjoyed its greatest period of prosperity. Subsequent generations were not so fortunate. The estate was sold during the mid-17th century and the mansion demolished a century or so later.

Places of Interest in the Neighbourhood
13. The Queen Eleanor Crosses (Geddington)
52. Bone of Contention (Stanion)
53. The Curious Custom of the 'Pole Fair' (Corby)
58. Monument to the Holy Trinity (Rushton)

70 Ancient Advertisements

Position: Gretton, Weldon and Collyweston.
OS Map: Kettering & Corby, Sheet 141.
Map Ref: SP897941, SP925893 and SK997028.
Access: Gretton stands 3 miles north of Corby on minor roads between Rockingham and Harringworth, off the A6003. Weldon is to the east of Corby, with Haunt Hill House due west of the church. Collyweston lies 3 miles south-west of Stamford on the A43.

Whilst many of Northamptonshire's curiosities are stamped with true eccentricity, a number employed unorthodox forms specifically to arouse attention. The inscribed stone of the Lamport bakehouse (see No 40) might be considered one example, and the stonemason's plaque to Aldwinkle (see No 57) another. Two others are to be found at Gretton and Weldon, with a third at Collyweston.

'Stonecroft' at Gretton was originally one of a pair of cottages built of local stone under a thatched roof. This has now been replaced with slates and its neighbour demolished. But it is the carved tablet beneath the roof eaves and immediately over the front door that really distinguishes it. At one time inhabited by a local stonemason, he probably included the plaque to demonstrate his abilities.

Haunt Hill House in Weldon was constructed by master mason Humphrey Frisby. Here, the south end is devoted to decorative features more usually associated with a stately home. Dating from 1636, it is conceivable that Frisby had worked on one of a number of great houses in the area, and may have used materials they had discarded.

At the 'Old Forge' in Collyweston, an over-sized horseshoe surrounds the gable window of the former blacksmith's shop. Built in the early 19th century on the main road through the village, the smithy must have been one of the busiest local concerns, providing tools for farmers and wheelwrights fittings as well as horseshoes.

Places of Interest in the Neighbourhood
Gretton and Weldon: 60. A Lighthouse in the Forest (Weldon)
   61. The Village Roundhouse (Weldon)
Collyweston: 74. Fragments Fit for a King (Collyweston)
   75. Pre-reformation Priests House (Easton-on-the-Hill)

The Old Forge at Collyweston.

The viaduct across the Welland Valley at Harringworth.

71 Sacrifice of the Picturesque

Position: Harringworth/Shotley.
OS Map: Kettering & Corby, Sheet 141.
Map Ref: SP913970 to SP914980 and SP925973.
Access: 5 miles north of Corby and 9 miles south-west of Stamford,
Harringworth may be reached from the A43 by heading west on the
minor road through Laxton and on towards the county boundary.
Shotley lies within ½ mile of Harringworth, on the north bound road to
Wakerley.

The building of the viaduct across the Wellend Valley immediately
to the west of Harringworth in the late 19th century undoubtedly
destroyed the valley's rural tranquillity. This immense structure of
some 82 colossal arches, constructed entirely with blue bricks, marches
for approximately 3/4 mile across the valley connecting Rutland and
beyond with the rail line to St. Pancras. Acclaimed as a spectacular
engineering achievement at the time, it dominates the western side of
the village. On its completion, the south-western view of the picturesque
valley was partially obscured with its massive legs almost standing in
the back gardens of more than one house. The national interests of
good rail links obviously outweighed any local objections, but successive generations now live with the consequences.

   A different view was taken at nearby Shotley, where, in a hamlet of no
more than eight properties, the 1860's owner of Shotley Cottage sought
permission to erect a Congregational chapel in Harringworth. The re-
quest was refused, but so determined was the cottage owner that he
sacrificed his own front garden, filling it with the small brick building
which still dominates the cottage today. After serving the community
for almost a century, the chapel closed as a place of worship in 1961.

Places of Interest in the Neighbourhood
1. Ancient Advertisements (Gretton)
2. The Solitary Statue (Blatherwyke)
3. 'Heels over Head' Burial (Blatherwyke)

72 The Solitary Statue

Position: Blatherwyke.
OS Map: Kettering & Corby, Sheet 141.
Map Ref: SP980957.
Access: About 7 miles north-east of Corby, Blatherwyke lies ½ mile to the east of the A43. Cross the bridge over Willow Brook and the entrance gates to the grounds are next to the first property on the left.

Near the summit of rising ground by a dirt track across open fields stands the lone figure of a man in Roman dress, surveying the view before him. This isolated piece of statuary, at times almost lost amidst crops, has a welcoming arm outstretched as if to invite the onlooker to share his majestic location. His lonely vigil is one of a number of reminders of the country house which once stood here.

Blatherwyke Hall was built in 1713 and owned by the Stafford and O'Brien families. It became empty during the Second World War, and was used by troops and prisoners of war. Much damage was caused, and in 1948 the Hall was sold and demolished.

On the bridge over Willow Brook and on the deer-keeper's cottage just past the carriage gates is the emblem of the Stafford and O'Brien families, comprising the Stafford knot with entwined initials. Passing through the gates into the former grounds, the large stable block with the lettering 'D. O'B. 1770' (Donatus O'Brien) can be seen. This last vestige of the estate buildings retains an air of decay in spite of its new-found use for commercial purposes. The drive runs parallel with the brook for some distance before turning away and rising to the statue in the fields. The view from here is of probably the most durable feature on the estate, the man-made lake said to have been hand dug by Irish labourers brought to Northamptonshire by the O'Briens at the time of the potato famine in Ireland.

Places of Interest in the Neighbourhood
70. Ancient Advertisements (Gretton, Collyweston)
71. Sacrifice of the Picturesque (Harringworth/Shotley)
73. 'Heels over Head' Burial (Blatherwyke)

73 'Heels over Head' Burial

Position: Blatherwyke.
OS Map: Kettering & Corby, Sheet 141.
Map Ref: SP972956.
Access: About 7 miles north-east of Corby, Blatherwyke lies within ½ mile to the east of the A43. Cross the brook and the former rectory is on the right.

Within the grounds of the former Blatherwyke Hall, standing on high ground near the former stable block, is the redundant church of the Holy Trinity.

In the nearby glebe land, sometime during the late 18th or early 19th century, two stone coffins were discovered. The larger of the two is about four feet long and contained human remains of what was thought to be a female corpse. The skeleton comprised only the bones from the knees upwards, as the remainder was found in the other coffin. This smaller container dated from Roman times and also contained a small urn. The origins of the skeleton have remained unproved, as have the

Roman stone coffins in the garden of the former Blatherwyke rectory.

circumstances in which she lost her lower legs, although this has attracted some speculation.

One theory suggested that the remains were those of Queen Bodicea who, whilst retreating from the Romans near St. Albans, may have been cut down by the rotating blades of a chariot's axle. In 1834 however, a similarly split skeleton was discovered beneath the floor of Hinchingbrook House, near Huntingdon, when flooring of the former priory was removed. This skeleton was believed to have been buried in the 16th century at the time of the Dissolution of the Monasteries and it seems likely that the Blatherwyke remains were of similar origin hastily buried in existing coffins. The small urn has remained the property of the church, while the stone coffins, in much the same arrangement as when they were buried, now decorate the terrace of the former rectory.

Places of Interest in the Neighbourhood
70. Ancient Advertisements (Gretton, Collyweston)
71. Sacrifice of the Picturesque (Harringworth/Shotley)
72. The Solitary Statue (Blatherwyke)

The sundial at Collyweston.

74 Fragments Fit for a King

Position: Collyweston.
OS Map: Kettering & Corby, Sheet 141.
Map Ref: SK994029.
Access: 3½ miles south-west of Stamford, Collyweston lies on the A43. Take the road signposted to Ketton and the curiosity may be seen within 150 yards on the left.

It is easy to dismiss this curious stump of masonry beside a narrow lane in Collyweston as the surviving chimney-stack of some long-since collapsed cottage. The inquisitive however will learn differently.

It sits within a high boundary wall, which conveniently has a gateless opening allowing access. Inside, is a sadly overrun garden, formerly maintained as public parkland, where further inspection of the 'chimney' reveals the sturdy remains of a large sundial. Three feet thick, ten feet wide and fifteen feet high, it is formed in an alcove of local stone with an arched and concave top. The hours are marked from 8.00 a.m. to 7.00 p.m., with each half and quarter hour also identified. The gnomon, which cast the shadow line, is unfortunately missing, although its former location can still be seen.

This immense time-piece dates from the early 16th century and stood on the terraced gardens of the palace which existed here. The palace itself was the home of Lord Cromwell, treasurer to King Henry VI, and later Margaret, the Countess of Richmond, whose son was to end the War of the Roses and launch the Tudors to power as Henry VII.

Various descriptions of the palace mention its size and grandeur, but alas, all has now gone. Some fragments may be seen incorporated in the nearby church of St. Andrew, where there are intricate carvings around door. Elsewhere a barn has an attached dovecote, a garden outhouse has a lozenge-shaped window built into it, and the remains of garden terracing with fishponds can be seen.

Places of Interest in the Neighbourhood
4. Ancient Advertisements (Collyweston)
5. Pre-Reformation Priest's House (Easton-on-the-Hill)
7. A Discarded Stately Home (Wothorpe)
8. An Unusual Funeral (Stamford Baron)

75 Pre-Reformation Priest's House

Position: Easton-on-the-Hill.
OS Map: Kettering & Corby, Sheet 141.
Map Ref: TF009046.
Access: Just 2 miles south-west of Stamford, Easton-on-the-Hill lies on the A43 from Corby. Heading north into the village, take the first left turn by the public house on the corner and continue in a straight line until the road bends slightly to the left. The Priest's House stands here, on the right.

In a county which is renowned for the quality and quantity of large houses belonging to the landed gentry it is curious that a smaller but not insignificant house isn't given greater acclaim. Built of local stone under a roof of Collyweston slates, it dates from the late 15th or early 16th century, and is a rare example of a pre-Reformation Priests House.

   Designed originally as a residence for the solitary and celibate clergy of the day, it possibly accommodated a priest and his wife following the Reformation. Mid-19th century descriptions refer to it as being used as a barn or stable, which is how it remained until the mid-20th century. In 1963 it was saved from demolition by the then incumbent and the Peterborough Society, who jointly fought for its purchase and restoration by the National Trust.

Places of Interest in the Neighbourhood
70. Ancient Advertisements (Collyweston)
74. Fragments Fit for a King (Collyweston)
77. A Discarded Stately Home (Wothorpe)
78. An Unusual Funeral (Stamford Baron)

The pre-Reformation priest's house at Easton-on-the-Hill.

76 The Curious County Boundary

Position: The Soke of Peterborough.
OS Map: Kettering & Corby, Sheet 141.
Peterborough, Sheet 142.
Map Ref: TF020058 and TL075982.

The county boundary of Northamptonshire has undergone numerous changes since the Treaty of Agreement between Alfred the Great and the occupying Danish armies in 878 AD. Then, Watling Street (the present A5) formed the dividing boundary, with the Danes to the east occupying much of what is now Northamptonshire in a district they named 'Hamtum'. It was they who thus gave the county its name, which first appears as 'Hamtanscir' on a document of 1011.

By the time of Doomsday Book in 1086 the familiar 70 x 20 miles south-west to north-east strip of land had generally become established as the county. Some further minor adjustments to its boundaries occured, but the area broadly remained unchanged for over eight centuries.The County Council's Act of 1888 eventually allowed ' the Soke of Peterborough' to sever its ancient connections, becoming a part of Huntingdonshire in 1965 and part of Cambridgeshire following the 1974 reorganisations. The new boundary crosses the old Wittering Airfield, south of Stamford, before rejoining the old boundary at Wansford.

From its initial 800 year period many notable curiosities remain and form a significant part of Northamptonshire's history. Four are included on the following pages.

Places of Interest in the Neighbourhood
77. A Discarded Stately Home (Wothorpe)
78. An Unusual Funeral (Stamford Baron)
79. The Architectural Curiosities of Milton Park
80. The Bishop's Sundial (Upton)

77 A Discarded Stately Home

Position: Wothorpe (The Soke of Peterborough).
OS Map: Kettering & Corby, Sheet 141.
Map Ref: TF024053.
Access: Wothorpe is signposted from the A43 between Stamford and
Easton-on-the-Hill, and may be approached from one direction only.
Follow the rough track at the end of the road for about 3/4 mile: the
ruins are in fields to the left.

During the 17th century, at approximately the same time as Burghley
House in the adjacent parish, Wothorpe Hall was built for Lord
Burghley's eldest son, Thomas Cecil, Earl of Exeter. Occupied for less
than a hundred years, it has been ruinous since the 18th century, having

Wothorpe Hall, ruinous since the 18th century.

now lost each of its four wings, but retaining much of its core. Most notably it consists of four corner towers, each square in plan and surmounted with octagonal turrets. Little of the external skin of the building remains, but in places flat swirls of decorative stonework are still evident. The forecourt was entered through a stepped entrance gateway which still survives to the north-east.

Places of Interest in the Neighbourhood
78. An Unusual Funeral (Stamford Baron)
79. The Architectural Curiosities of Milton Park
80. The Bishop's Sundial (Upton)

78 An Unusual Funeral

Position: Stamford Baron (The Soke of Peterborough).
OS Map: Kettering & Corby, Sheet 141.
Map Ref: TF031068.
Access: The churchyard of St. Martin's in Stamford Baron lies just off the A47 and B1443 to Barnack. The church fronts the main road through the town with the churchyard at the rear, across the road and past the gates.

The oddest of the curiosities within the Soke of Peterborough must be the modest gravestone which stands in the churchyard of St. Martin's, identifying the grave of Daniel Lambert. In 1809, Lambert attended the local races, lodging at the Wagon and Horses Inn. On a June morning he died in his room, thus posing something of a problem to both the landlord and undertakers called to remove his corpse – for Daniel Lambert weighed 52 stone. In the end one wall of the inn had to be demolished. His coffin was built on wheels and hauled by twenty men. A ramp was dug down into his grave, along which the coffin was rolled to its final resting place. The tombstone bears the following inscription:

In Remembrance of that Prodigy in Nature Daniel Lambert
a Native of Leicester who was possessed of an exalted and
convivial Mind and in personal Greatness had no Competitor.
He measured three Feet one Inch round the Leg
nine Feet four Inches round the Body
and weighed Fifty Two Stone Eleven Pounds
He departed this Life on the 21st of June 1809
Aged 39 Years

As a Testimony of Respect this stone is erected by his Friends in Leicester

Places of Interest in the Neighbourhood
77. A Discarded Stately Home (Wothorpe)
79. The Architectural Curiosities of Milton Park
80. The Bishop's Sundial (Upton)

79 The Architectural Curiosities of Milton Park

Position: Milton Park (The Soke of Peterborough).
OS Map: Peterborough, Sheet 142.
Map Ref: TL153995 and TL150988.
Access: 1 ½ miles west of Peterborough, Milton Park lies immediately north of the A47 with both follies in the grounds of the Hall. Viewing by prior arrangement with the Agent, Milton Park Estate Office, Milton Park, Peterborough.

During the late-14th century the Abbot of Peterborough was granted rights to hunt the royal forests in the area by Richard II. The pack of hounds established then was later given to the Fitzwilliam family who have lived at Milton since 1500. The pack remains one of only three so-called 'Governing Packs', from which most others have been bred. The original kennels were destroyed by fire in the 19th century and relocated in the present sham ruin which dates from 1767. It is thought by some to have been designed by Sir William Chambers, and was built as a medieval gatehouse, with a tall castellated tower, squat, heavy buttressing, and a pointed arch entrance gate, set in a high wall with arrow-slit windows.

   A second folly in the grounds is the small High Gothic lodge, per-haps by either Humphrey Repton or John Nash. Here an impressive rose window sits below a gabled frieze similar to that at Peterborough Cathedral. Octagonal in plan, it also features elegant arches, pinnacled buttresses and a quite splendid setting.

Places of Interest in the Neighbourhood
77. A Discarded Stately Home (Wothorpe)
78. An Unusual Funeral (Stamford Baron)
80. The Bishop's Sundial (Upton)

The Gothic Lodge at Milton Park

The sundial/calendar at Upton in the Soke of Peterborough.

80 The Bishop's Sundial

Position: Upton (The Soke of Peterborough).
OS Map: Peterborough, Sheet 142.
Map Ref: TF110006.
Access: Upton is 4 miles west of Peterborough to the north of the A47.
Continue through the village towards the manor house at the far end:
the sundial is on the left.

As may be seen from the examples at Collyweston and Weekley (No's
74 and 50) sundials attained great prominence through their size.
During the reign of Elizabeth I, however, they became more complex,
and the one at Upton is a rare example of the sundial at its most
sophisticated. It was designed by Bishop Dove of Peterborough, and
combined both sundial and calendar, indicating religious festivals and
other significant days, such as midwinter. Sadly, its condition has
deteriorated. All but the boldest of the marks have eroded, leaving the
onlooker to wonder at how such a curiously hollowed piece of stone
could once have achieved so much.

Places of Interest in the Neighbourhood
77. A Discarded Stately Home (Wothorpe)
78. An Unusual Funeral (Stamford Baron)
79. The Architectural Curiosities of Milton Park

Index

Places by Page Number

The Curiosities of England

The following titles in the series have already been published and can be ordered at all bookshops, or in case of difficulties direct from the publishers.